PROPHETIC ENGAGEMENT

The Issachar Mandate

UNLOCKING THE HIDDEN POWER OF
THE INTERPRETIVE FUNCTION
IN THE GIFT OF PROPHECY

OBII PAX-HARRY

DESTINY IMAGE® EUROPE
Via Maiella, 1
66020 San Giovanni Teatino (Ch) - Italy

ISBN 10: 88-89127-31-7
ISBN 13: 978-88-89127-31-5

For Worldwide Distribution. Printed in Italy.

1 2 3 4 5 6 7 8/10 09 08 07 06

This book and all other Destiny Image Europe books are available at Christian bookstores and distributors worldwide.

To order products, or for any other correspondence:

DESTINY IMAGE® EUROPE
Via Acquacorrente, 6
65123 - Pescara - Italy
Tel. +39 085 4716623 - Fax: +39 085 4716622
E-mail: info@eurodestinyimage.com

Or reach us on the Internet:
www.eurodestinyimage.com

DEDICATION

In memory of my beloved mother Esther Ejiogu who taught me to pray without ceasing. I still have two black spots on my knees from our many hours of prayer. Thank you, mama, for your life led in self-less service to our family, and to the Lord. Thank you for your stories of angels in your bedroom.

Thank you for being my mother and friend!

Until we meet again, you will be forever in my heart.

Acknowledgments

I would like to thank my best friend and my husband, Dr. Pax, a most honorable man who has selflessly supported me over the years in ministry. Also to our children, Data, Daye, and Daibi, thanks for your sacrifice; your smiling faces make it all the more worthwhile.

I would also like to thank my assistants and friends, Jenny Lloyd and Deborah Smith, for loyalty and commitment to this project.

Obii Pax-Harry
December 2004

ENDORSEMENTS

This book helps the prophetic gift shift into a new gear. It challenges and thrills as it draws on very broad and deep scriptural reference to relocate the prophetic calling fully into the context for which it was given, "that believers today start to exercise prophecy as a matter of mission." And it empowers the reader to dare to go there!

Sue Mitchell
Coauthor of *Target Europe*
Cofounder, Passion Europe

I first met Obii Pax-Harry through a minister/friend on my staff. Obii later became involved in our international apostolic women's network (WIMN) as a woman leader in England. She is a brilliant strategist, intercessor, prophet to the nations, and minister of the Gospel. It doesn't surprise me that Obii would have a special word for this season in the Body of Christ. May we all be awakened to the signs of the times and fulfill our God-given mandates.

Dr. Sharon Predovitch
Co-Pastor, Resurrection Life Church & World Ministry Center
Minneapolis, Minnesota, U.S.A.

Divine connections are essential if we're to discover the true "hearing" and "seeing" in the Spirit of God for these days. Kerry and I experienced that "divine connection" when we met Obii Pax-Harry for the first time a few years ago.

Obii and her team at Women Arise have consistently spoken into the ministry of Cross Rhythms with accuracy and thus great spiritual encouragement, which has been vital for the team as we have pursued righteous broadcasting.

"Words are the garments that clothe our thoughts" and this "honesty of transparency" is an essential quality, especially for the prophetic gift among us, to ensure the prophetic gift is really speaking on behalf of God. We have found a great integrity within Obii's life to pursue this reconciliation of accuracy.

Chris and Kerry Cole
Founders, Cross Rhythms

CONTENTS

FOREWORD

There are many good books that cover different aspects of the gift of prophecy. There are also books that help us understand the ministry and role of the prophet. *Prophetic Engagement* is not simply another book on prophecy. Yes, there is teaching within the book that addresses necessary foundational issues surrounding the gifts of the Spirit and how they can be profitably exercised. There is also some very good solid material on the ministry of the prophet. Those parts of the book alone would call for *Prophetic Engagement* to be read. If Obii had simply addressed those issues I would have wholeheartedly said "read this book" as she writes clearly, with conviction, and always as one calling us forward. However, *Prophetic Engagement* is much more than a good book on prophecy and prophets that can be recommended.

I have known Obii for a number of years. When she speaks or writes I always take note. She has a unique understanding related to timings. For example, it was through her that I first had to consider the issue of "out-of-time wars." (You will read about that understanding in the pages that follow.)

There is much depth in this book and I suggest keeping *Prophetic Engagement* with you and going back over it repeatedly. Obii's understanding of timings, timelines for nations, and how boundaries work are three other aspects I have especially taken note of. You will highlight interesting aspects as well.

Obii truly carries her burdens faithfully. It is from that place, the place of intimacy, that her revelation flows. The revelation she brings accords closely to the Issachar anointing. I have heard her speak with deep insight relating to times, and even dates, and I know that as the words have been received there has been a clear call to action. She manifests in our time the Issachar anointing and prophetic engagement.

I have no hesitation in recommending this book. It should be read by as many people as possible: it needs to be read by mature prophets, by aspiring young believers, by pastors, and by those in the workplace. It should be read by individuals as well as groups of people who could work through the implications together. I have no doubt it will shape many lives and help contribute to the absolutely vital release of the Issachar anointing and prophetic engagement. We are in a time of cosmic turmoil, but there is a way through. The way through is not only a way of survival, but a way of victory. It is not a pathway without pain, but it is a pathway that will lead the Body of Christ to a higher place of revelation—and a deeper place of intimacy.

Finally, for those who know my own journey, my family is deeply grateful to Obii. She has proved to be a faithful friend, a prophet, a warrior to us, as indeed she and her team have been to many. I believe as you read this book you will find something of her overcoming spirit touching you too. I am grateful to the Lord for the gifts within the Body at this time. I am, and I am sure you will be, grateful for this book. Let the *Prophetic Engagement* be received, for it has been released from Heaven and is available in this wonderful hour of opportunity.

Martin Scott
Author, *Gaining Ground and Impacting the City*
Leatherhead, February 2006

INTRODUCTION

The sons of Issachar who had understanding of the times, to know what Israel ought to do (1 Chronicles 12:32).

The new role of the prophetic church calls for greater function of interpretative skills resident in the original tribe of Issachar. The prophetic church needs to identify more with present global issues, helping the world interpret ever-increasing natural disasters for instance. The Church as a prophetic community also bears the responsibility to serve the unsaved world by employing all divine abilities granted by Heaven. Prophets must help the rest of the world understand present fulfillment of prophecies—or not. Our world has seen more wars in recent times than ever recorded, with social injustice increasing almost on a daily basis. The current globalization process grants no room for an ineffective church that holds her soldiers inactive in times of combat.

Prophetic Engagement, The Issachar Mandate is a call to the prophetic church to reposition the gift of prophecy from almost predominantly "predictive" emphasis to an "interpretative" role. There is a call for mobile prophetic. The gift of foresight and forth telling needs to shift to our streets—or at least overflow into the marketplace. This mandate is also to be received as a clarion call to the prophetic church to engage more proactively with Christian media; to stand in incessant intercession for the rising of a global righteous broadcasting army. The Lord's call to the Church to perceive the need for an apostolic and prophetic Christian media army is urgent. Now is the time to mass communicate the voice of God across the earth (see Matt. 24:14).

On a recent tour to Israel, I received several open visions of key ministries placing their satellites on a hill in Jerusalem. The ministries I saw were not solely broadcasting organizations but were a representation of the entire Church. My understanding from the Lord was that a time would come when the Church will need to broadcast the good news of His Gospel from the holy hills of Jerusalem. Although I was being shown *spiritual* Jerusalem, *natural* Jerusalem would be key in a time of communication boost needing interpreters. This is that time when the Church must prepare for repositioning. While on the same tour, and at a crucial time outside of the garden of Gethsamene, I received an open vision of the New Jerusalem. The entire city stood beautifully colored over a hill in the distance. To my surprise, this time in a dream, I saw the same picture of the New Jerusalem on the same hill. It was no longer standing over the hill; it rested *on* the hill. The urgency of the times we live in need to be interpreted.

Prophetic Engagement is a call to the prophetic community to interpret the times of God to a world that has half its population living in abject poverty. But most importantly, this message aims to raise and equip an army who can respond to the call of the Spirit with an emphatic, *"Here am I! send me"* (Isa. 6:8). I have attempted to share the burden of my heart for a church that is not to serve under pressure of being culturally relevant but one that must offload the culture of Heaven.

The objectives of the Kingdom cannot be achieved except the entire Body of Christ is released. I have often been fascinated by the fact that we seem to avoid the Scriptures that make for easy fulfillment of divine purposes. So, I have written with the concern of my heart that if some within the Body are to equip others for the work of the ministry, we need to find out who and where they are. To my mind, there seem to be enough reasons to earnestly discover the trainers and training gifts among us so those who must be trained can receive the necessary preparation to fulfill their own destiny.

I am aware of the fact that the fivefold functions are in partial operation; but so far, it would be fair to humbly admit, partial abilities have not worked well for the Church. A power house unable to give off enough energy leaves its subscribers with half electricity current. I am equally surprised that the Church fails to adopt the obvious principle set out in apostle Paul's teaching in Ephesians 2:20-22. We need the apostles and prophets to set firm foundations so the house of God can stand as designed. This is the cause of the Issachar Mandate—a clarion call to arms.

Obii Pax-Harry
February 2006

Chapter One

⊷ ⊱⊰ ⊶

BRIDGING GAPS

10/23/08

7/20/21

Jesus Christ fulfilled the Old Testament prophets and prophecies in body and ministry. He did not abrogate the past; He stood as fulfillment of the past, thereby bridging gaps in time, in order to point to the future. For thousands of years prophets of old like Isaiah and Daniel spoke of the Messiah to come. Old Testament types and shadows pointed to His identity as Messiah, as Saviour. When He came, the Jews were disappointed as His humble state did not meet with their expectations of a Messiah as King of the Jews. Their understanding of the kingdom He taught was of an external, physical domain, but Jesus disappointed the Pharisees when He announced the Kingdom of God did not come by observation[1] because it is an internal experience[2].

Jesus declared, *"Do not think that I came to destroy the Law or the Prophets. I did not come to destroy but to fulfill"* (Matt. 5:17). He came as "what is," in order to bridge the gap between "what was" and "what was to come." He is the same yesterday, today, and forever. Through his birth, Jesus brought completion to the partial revelation of the old that referred to what was to come; Jesus, the

Messiah. Again, the past and the present merged into one new era in Christ as Jesus fulfilled messianic prophecies, in part. The implication for the future meant every word of prophecy pointing to the Messiah to come received new status as "fulfilled." At His second coming all other prophecy will be fulfilled.

This is the testimony Jesus bore when he said, *"For assuredly, I say to you, till heaven and earth pass away, one jot or one tittle will by no means pass from the law till all is fulfillled"* (Matt. 5:18). Jesus became the bridge between the past and the future. In his supremacy as the Messiah, Jesus became the *figure* for future reference, no longer a shadow to be interpreted. He became a sign pointing to the future of which we have now become stakeholders (Matt. 28:18).

In times of transition, such as the global Body of Christ is experiencing, interpretative skills of the children of Issachar need to be engaged so that believers and unbelievers alike receive understanding of changing trends. The children of Issachar were men *"who had understanding of the times, to know what Israel ought to do"* (1 Chron. 12:32). The entire Body of saints needs to function in common understanding of paradigms of seasonal changes. Everyone deserves to know whether the Church and our world are indeed experiencing change or not.

It is no longer enough to hear such pronouncements from our pulpits or Christian television programs. We must now interpret and give language to the alleged changes. I use the word "alleged" loosely—not doubting the infallibility of God's Word, but in humble recognition of man's inadequacies. Misinterpretation of spiritual change can hinder future progress. The case of the Jerusalem Council and the revival of the Gentile population lends to my argument[3]. The fact of the free gift of salvation proved too much for legalists who sought to mix the old and new. Their message read, *"Unless you are circumcised according to the custom of Moses, you cannot be saved"* (Acts 15:1). The new phenomenon, a pivotal change and a departure from the old mind-set needed interpreting.

James stood in the place and position which the message of Issachar Mandate proclaims. He engaged and interpreted the words of a prophet of old—Amos[4] whose prophecy pointed to the future that was being fulfilled in the Gentiles who received salvation. James bridged the gap between past words of Amos and present-day fulfillment[5] in order that strategy for future advancement may be deduced. The apostles, elders, and the whole Church came to common agreement on the way forward[6].

An apostolic team made up of *"men who have risked their lives for the name of our Lord Jesus Christ"*[7] were entrusted with the responsibility of assessing the situation. Among the team were *"Judas and Silas, themselves being prophets also, [who] exhorted and strengthened the brethren with many words"* (Acts 15:32). More than ever the Body of Christ is being called to communicate clearly and efficiently the truth of the Gospel and its relevance in this age. Several Scriptures speak of the signs of the end of the ages[8] and of pursuant confusion in people not grounded in sound doctrine.[9] The Bible relates directly and indirectly the competition of the last days between false and true doctrine, false and true prophets.[10] The interpretative function of the prophetic gift in operation empowers effective evangelism in our time.

Timing is so important to fulfilling destiny.[11] Assume, for instance, someone had an appointment at a set time, but arrived late having misread the time on their wrist watch. Two things can result from such an error of timing. First, the meeting may be aborted because the person who read the time right had no one to meet with. Second, if the the person showed up late, due to the constrained timing, the quality of discussion or agreement may be compromised. Similarly, the Church must realize how critical timing is, become engaged, and urgently pursue the Issachar Mandate—to interpret words that currently leave us with too many options, but not enough understanding to make the right choices in God.

Through Bible history and experience, the interpretative gift alluded to the tribe of Issachar can be said to emerge naturally in people in covenant with God. At times of pivotal change God often stirs hunger for understanding and interpretation of expectancy felt in the natural. Through supernatural understanding of the times Simeon[12] and

Anna[13] prepared for the coming of the Messiah in prayer and fasting.[14] Daniel divinely received understanding of the time for the end of Israel's captivity. Another prophet Jeremiah spoke of such a time[15] but when it arrived, supernatural insight unlocked past history for present-day fulfillment of words prophesied[16] (Dan. 9:2). Now as new creation believers, we are predisposed to interpretative grace, an important function of the prophetic gift (1 Chron. 12:32). The Spirit of God stirs in believers the ability to understand the times and to know what the Church and nations ought to do in times of pivotal change. I believe we are in the beginning of a new age to usher in Christ's return.

Issachar anointing enables accurate interpretation of changing spiritual trends and natural manifestations of such changes. Imagine if Jesus Christ simply arrived in Nazareth with no history, announcing to the Jews, "Guess what, I have come into town to take up position as the Son of God, your Saviour, your only hope of everlasting life; and by the way, I have no parents or lineage. I was just sent by my Father, so call me 'Sent'." The Israelites would have plotted the crucifixion earlier than history records.

But God in his infinite wisdom fulfilled the words of his messengers in His Son Jesus Christ's birth, ministry, death, and resurrection. In other words, Jesus gave meaning to the words spoken in times past. He became a sign leading to the future.[17] For hundreds of years before the Lord's coming, the prophets had ceased functioning, but the spirit of Elijah was to usher in an era of repentance and reconciliation (Mal. 4:6). John the Baptist came in the spirit of Elijah to bridge a gap and to prepare a people for the day of the Lord. His mission included "to give knowledge of salvation to His people."[18] I believe the people who lived in John's time could understand by human sight but he was to usher them into spiritual perception by interpreting the essence of salvation.

TIME FOR SAINTS TO POSSESS THE KINGDOM

Once more the Spirit of God, the spirit of Elijah, is manifesting through the saints to make ready a remnant people for Kingdom dwelling. We need to assume our prophetic role as interpreters of present-day truth.

About four years ago, I saw an amazing picture of a throne and paraphernalia of a court room in magnificence. When I inquired of the Lord to understand details of the open vision I received during our church prayer meeting, I was led to Daniel 7:

> *I was watching; and the same horn was making war against the saints, and prevailing against them, until the Ancient of Days came, and a judgement was made in favor of the saints of the Most High, and **the time came for the saints to possess the kingdom**"* (verses 21-22, author's emphasis).

The courtroom I saw was of the Ancient of Days; and the scene was of His court in session.[19] The Lord was dressed in white with a golden band across His waist. As the vision unfolded, I inquired of the Lord; to know what He was doing. He responded, *"Judging the enemies of My people."* I watched as cancer, arthritis, AIDS, poverty, and all manner of sickness were called up, and judged. Each disease, difficulty, and challenge was called up by name in the category of *"every high thing that exalts itself against the knowledge of God"* (2 Cor. 10:5) to answer to the Ancient of Days. The verdict was read: *"and the time came for the saints to possess the kingdom"* (Dan. 7:22). I received this vision in 2002 and our pastor asked me to share it with the church. We rejoiced then but now, with benefit of Issachar anointing and the encouragement of prophetic engagement, I believe the Body of Christ is to live the reality of the joy we felt in 2002.

The power of the Kingdom of God will not manifest through one or two ministries but in a broader sense. This reality needs to be translated so all are ready for the "suddenly" surge of God's power—but not until the dynamics unfolding are interpreted. We achieve when all understand. This is the message that *Prophetic Engagement, The Issachar Mandate* desires to communicate.

INTERPRETING ISLAM'S THREAT

A few months before the vision of the Ancient of Days, I was taken in the spirit on February 2, 2002, and given a document titled, "Word for the Decade and Beyond"[20] containing insight of world events until 2012. Two significant prophecies recorded for 2004 were: "a disaster that would occur in East Asia affecting the economy," and the "death of Arafat." The Middle East shift revealed as a "surprise twist" in the prophetic herald can now be interpreted as a "suddenly" of God. President Arafat died in November 2004, and the tsunami in the Indian Ocean occurred in December 2004.

To bring the events documented for 2004 into fulfillment, the Lord revealed Himself in another open vision at the beginning of November 2004. He was dressed as Jehovah Saboath,[21] Man of War. The Lord stood over Jerusalem with His shining sword raised up in the air as though ready for war (Isa. 59:15-21). About a week later, President Arafat died. The Lord spoke to my heart to tell His people not to fear over Islam because He had taken its head just as David did Goliath (1 Sam. 17:51). The Lord wants the Church to be concerned with manifesting His glory, the glory of His Kingdom (Isa. 60:1-3). *The Enemy is distracting the Saints w/2 many Negatives*

INTERPRETING THE TSUNAMI OF DECEMBER 26, 2004

During September 2004, I received a telephone invitation to minister in India in April 2005. Before the end of the conversation Pastor Paul asked that I pray and prophesy into his nation. I only received one word from the Lord for India and neighboring nations: *"I see flooding that would be similar to the days of Noah, and this is imminent, unless the church prayed."* I remember the closing words of the prophecy were, *"The Lord has declared war against the millions of gods."* The Lord revealed His war was against His enemies—false gods. On December 14, 2004, the Lord stirred my spirit to prophesy a *"clash of kingdoms"* had occurred on that day. I remember my assistants and I praying throughout the day to discern the obvious disturbances in the spiritual climate that we felt were relevant to our immediate environment. It was not until the prayer meeting on Tuesday, December 14 when the <u>Lord revealed a clash of His Kingdom and the kingdom of darkness</u>. On Sunday, December 19, during our Sunday worship time, I suddenly felt a divine unction to speak out, but I was unprepared for what the Lord revealed. His words to our assembly of worshipers were: *"a clash of kingdoms has occurred and this will be confirmed through a cosmic sign upon the earth seven days from today."*

True to His Word the tsunami was reported exactly seven days after December 19, 2004, when the Lord warned the Church. Because of the earthquake and resulting tsunami the economy of East Asia was adversely affected—as revealed in the 2002 document.

Should I be celebrated as a great prophet or prophetess? No, the Lord is to be celebrated as a Great God. Prophetic engagement and the Issachar Mandate is for right perspectives so the Church becomes more accurate, not so individuals become more famous.

I was in Washington, D.C., totally oblivious of the tsunami news, until the Lord spoke to me in a dream on December 29 revealing "India needs you." My friend Rev. Eva Alexander telephoned to confirm that she tried to warn the church in India, and mobilize prayer in obedience to the Word of the Lord, *"unless the Church prayed."* My spirit agonized as I read newspaper headlines and listened to so many broadcasts with the recurring question: "where was God"? Several testimonies of the mercy of God emerged from survivors of the tsunami but the secular media preferred news that left many questioning the mercy of our God.

Jenny Lloyd, one of my assistants, had received insight from the Lord in October 2004, that one of the prophecies for that year was about to be fulfillled. She and Debbie Smith rummaged for weeks through our archives to find a copy of "Word for the Decade and Beyond," the booklet based on my vision of prophecies covering world events from 2002 until 2012. I am often pleased by God's humbling discipleship of the prophet's spirit. A true prophetic ministry is never able to celebrate the ovation of accuracy; the glory goes to the Lord.

The Church needs to come into maturity of her responsibility to interpret the signs of the end of the age as they unfold. We cannot vindicate God, but we are able to evangelize the world by preaching the truth of the Word of God, including the imminence of His return[22] and the signs that point to the beginning of such an age (see Matt. 24:14).

MIND THE GAP

When Jesus completed His assignment on earth He did not leave any gaps. He transferred "all" authority that had been given to Him "*in heaven and on earth*" to His disciples who were to stand as "continuation" of His ministry (see Matt. 28:18-19). This time, the disciples stood in a different capacity: *not as fulfillment of prophecy* like Jesus, but as *continuation or extension* of Jesus Christ. Their job was not to "stand" as fulfillment, but to "interpret" manifestations of a new epoch. This assignment connected the early church with the society they were to change. They had truth to broadcast, false doctrines to challenge, and spiritual terrorists to destroy.[23] Their new role involved interpreting paradigms to members of the Body who were stuck in an old mind-set (see Acts 15:6-35). Without clarity of communication, vision could be aborted or rudely interrupted. Interpretation of "change" allows for continuity of vision: "*Every good gift and every perfect gift is from above, and comes down from the Father of lights, with whom there is no variation or shadow of turning*" (James 1:17). The call of the Issachar Mandate is for the church to "arise" and actively engage once more to interpret changing trends of a new epoch.

It's our job to do.

It was the responsibility of the apostles and disciples to interpret teachings of Jesus Christ on principles of the Kingdom of God by living out practically the words of His teachings. They gave life to the Lord's words by becoming the "Word in action" through their ministries of signs, miracles, and wonders. Of the Kingdom of God Jesus taught, "*The law and the prophets were until John. Since that time the kingdom of God has been preached, and everyone is pressing into it*" (Luke 16:16). He revealed, "*the kingdom of God does not come with observation…Indeed the kingdom of God is within you*" (Luke 17:20-21). Jesus warned us not to react like the Pharisees in expecting an external kingdom. The Kingdom of which He taught was spiritual and internal, inside all believers. He cautioned, *"The kingdom of heaven suffers violence, and the violent take it by force"* (Matt. 11:12). The Kingdom of God manifests through tenacious saints. / like that

So in effect, the accomplishments of the early church not only confirmed the Lord's teachings but became the bridge connecting words and action. The commitment and tenacity with which the apostles and disciples preached and taught Kingdom principles yielded fruit from the onset. When Peter spoke shortly after the outpouring of God's Spirit to interpret the manifestations of the new phenomenon to onlookers *"that day about three thousand souls were added to them"* (Acts 2:41).

The unsaved in our communities need to understand natural changes so visible in our world today in order to respond to a spiritual call from the words of John 3:3, *"Most assuredly, I say to you, unless one is born again, he cannot see the kingdom of God."*

THE NICODEMUS SYNDROME

There are still many Nicodemuses in our time: people who need assistance of interpreted language to understand spiritual dynamics. Personally I am grateful for the gift of salvation because I would have been a Nicodemus, wanting to make sense of the package before tasting its contents. In vulnerability Nicodemus asked of the Lord Jesus: *"How can a man be born when he is old? Can he enter a second time into his mother's womb and be born"* (John 3:4).

Jesus then breaks down the revelation of salvation so that Nicodemus can make an informed decision. Obviously fascinated by a concept that does not make natural sense, Nicodemus again questioned, *"How can these things be?"* (John 3:9). The dialogue carried on with Jesus humbly breaking down the greatest gift of all:

For God so loved the world that He gave His only begotten Son, that whoever believes in Him should not perish but have everlasting life (John 3:16).

The Church needs language to interpret and communicate efficiently to many worldwide seeking answers. Expectations of the secular world and options open to the global Church of Christ are some of the issues at the core of the clarion call of prophetic engagement—the Issachar Mandate.

THE POWER IS IN THE MANTLE

Jesus transferred His mantle to the disciples, but its power and potency could not be realized until the Holy Spirit was poured out on them (see Matt. 24:49 and Acts 1:8). In fulfillment of the Lord's pronouncement, the Holy Spirit fell upon 120 faithful disciples who waited in an Upper Room in prayer for the moment of empowerment. Each of the apostles and disciples had a destiny to fulfill, local, national, and international spheres to impact with the Gospel of the Kingdom. Together they would change the world (see Acts 17:6).

Upon the outpouring of the Holy Spirit, every person present received a new identity. Evidence of personal transformation was related to numerous impossible tasks that became attainable. This pattern was evident in the Old Testament. When the *"Spirit of God"* was poured out, they became "new" persons. A sign of Saul's anointing as king of Israel was to come by way of the Spirit's transformation. Samuel, the spokesman of God, said to him, *"Then the Spirit of the Lord will come upon you, and you will prophesy with them and be turned into another man"* (1 Sam. 10:6). After David's anointing, *"the Spirit of the Lord came upon David from that day forward"* (1 Sam. 16:13). At the same time *"the Spirit of the Lord departed from Saul, and a distressing spirit from the Lord troubled him"* (1 Sam. 16:14). Saul attracted judgment for rebellion by a distressing spirit invading his soul.

30

Not by Power nor by Might

The empowering purpose of the Spirit's touch in the Old Testament was seen also in the life of Samson, the man of strength raised with a divine mandate to judge the Philistines. It is recorded that *"the Spirit of the Lord came mightily upon him, and he tore the lion apart as one would have torn apart a young goat, though he had nothing in his hand"* (Judg. 14:6). Can you imagine tearing a lion apart with your bare hands? This Bible narrative makes ripping apart goats sound like killing a mosquito. Even at that, modern technology has thankfully made mosquito killing an easy feat.

Such was the impact of *"a touch"* of the Spirit of God who dwells inside us. In other words, if the power that now *"dwells"* inside of every new creation believer could turn men *"upon"* whom the Spirit fell into gladiators, our prayer meetings should make angels sweat with activity. On another occasion, when the Spirit of the Lord came upon Samson he freed himself from the Philistine's bondage and slew 1,000 of their men with a fresh jawbone of a donkey (Judg. 15:14-15). In the time of Moses, the Spirit that was upon him was imparted on 70 men appointed as elders of Israel as a sign of ordination. When the Spirit rested upon them *"they prophesied, although they never did so again"* (Num. 11:25).

A Fresh Call

There is a fresh call on the Church as a prophetic community to position herself not only for a facelift, but for a complete transformation for Kingdom purposes. There is a new role for the prophetic church requiring us to function in the discernment of the tribe of Issachar. The Church must be fully conversant with spiritual timing and natural implications thereof (1 Chron. 12:32). The prophetic gift on the tribe of Issachar earned them a place in David's mighty army. In order for the Body of Christ to fulfill this call, the prophetic engagement calls for a spiritual repositioning of our prophetic gifts from inside church buildings to the streets outside.

The nature of prophecy makes the gift both predictive and interpretative. But the Church has preferred (and, I believe, exhausted) the predictive side to prophecy. We must now seek to function in more of the interpretative role of prophecy, helping those around us to make sense of natural disasters, cosmic signs, and other unusual occurrences in our world. Simply declaring Scriptures is no longer enough—now the Church must learn to interpret the Word of the Lord so that the unsaved understand the hope in Christ. Unravelling the Word of God through interpretative skills and making its essence applicable to our present times is the sole responsibility of the prophetic community. This is Prophetic Engagement and the Issachar Mandate!

"Go near and overtake this chariot" (Acts 8:29).

Philip, the disciple, was instructed by the angel of the Lord. He was supernaturally transformed into a mobile church to interpret the Scriptures to a man of authority. But first Philip had to be repositioned. An angel of the Lord spoke to him saying, *"Arise and go toward the south along the road which goes down from Jerusalem to Gaza"* (Acts 8:26). The Bible records this area as being a "desert" region. Philip went to the man who was in a desert-type spiritual climate bringing the fertile Word of God. The most uncommon sight in a desert is food.

Reading words that make no sense for lack of understanding is similar to life in a desert with no hope for food. When Philip heard the man reading Isaiah's words he asked the Ethiopian eunuch if he understood the words he was reading. The eunuch's response is the question the world is asking of the Church: *"How can I, unless someone guides me?"* (Acts 8:31). Philip bridged the gap by interpreting the words of a prophet of old to bring present- day application. The effect was seen in the resoluteness of the eunuch to be baptized. Jesus does not need to be marketed in fancy clothes—the truth and nothing but the truth is the only key to fulfilling our commission to the world. But first, the Church must covet supernatural force to overtake the chariots of humanism, secularism, Islam, and anti-Semitism.

The prophetic community needs to activate the transforming power of the Holy Spirit within each believer—now. More tunnels of supernatural understanding ought to be opened in readiness for the unsaved. In changing the mind-set of the corporate Body of Christ, many will be spiritually repositioned to serve causes close to the heart of God. We are to engage more with social injustice in our communities, with fresh insight for poverty alleviation. The Church was never meant to function like a "maintenance garage;" but we are to be the creative house of God, *"the pillar and ground of the truth"* (1 Tim. 3:15). Our function is not to maintain ideas created by secular think tanks or to clone ideas from the world in a bid to attract numbers to our buildings. The flesh manifests through striving, and the Spirit manifests through transforming power of the Lord (Rom. 12:1-2). The Spirit and the flesh are diametrically opposed; they are at war with each other (Gal. 5:16).

WHERE ARE THE PROPHETS?

Prophets need to be at the forefront of this revolution to see greater release of prophetic expressions in the Church. New sounds release language and with language, new expressions of God's heart are released. Prophetic initiatives targeted at youth cultures should receive wider support if the Church is to see a new generation arise for Christ. Believers are being summoned under the Issachar Mandate and prophetic engagement to function as a people with insight and foresight. As mentioned previously, prophecy has been exercised largely in its predictive nature but now a fresh role demands a change of function. It is important for the prophetic community to govern the manifold wisdom of Christ in an Issachar-type interpretative mantle. Topical issues, especially disasters, receive far-reaching media coverage. Often television viewers are subjected to rapid-response-type opinions from broadcasters whose task would usually demand interpretation of the news items. It would be beneficial for all to experience insight from prophets not robed in religious gowns.

Prophetic engagement is an urgent, revolutionary summons for a repositioning of the gift of prophecy. People on our streets and in our neighborhoods need to hear the voice of God. Presidents of nations would benefit from a prophetic community that understands the times. More government agencies, such as the police, will seek assistance from the Church over unresolved security matters.

The Church has wasted precious time bickering over doctrinal, theological, racial, and gender issues. The time to expend our energies criticizing one another's use of spiritual gifts has elapsed. Some prophetic streams reject the prefacing of prophecy with "thus says the Lord," others welcome the prefacing. An unfortunate effect of divisions plays itself out in the description of churches. Some are called "white churches," others "black churches;" beyond the racial lines of division are smaller segmenting. In Britain there is the "Nigerian church," and the "Australian church." It gets worse as one hears of churches established on basis of continent sections, regions, and any other comfort zone we can find. Satan, our adversary, enjoys contentions. He is probably amused by the thought of a divided army intending to unseat his citadels, altars of evil, and thrones of iniquity (Matt. 12:5).

The time has come to recognize any gaps existing in understanding of prophetic gifting. Unless such gaps are closed through teaching, believers will be robbed of tools for practical outworking of our spiritual gift. The Lord Jesus stood as the fulfillment of prophecy and the Law[24] while his followers served as manifestations of his teachings. The Body of Christ is required in this prophetic hour to stand as interpreters and translators of prophetic signs of our time. The fact of the matter is that the role of the Church as a prophetic community with responsibilities to society needs to be interpreted so that the entire army of believers are adequately prepared for the tasks at hand. It is vital that every member of the Body of Christ appreciate our corporate and individual accountability in terms of societal needs. The time has come for the Church to "self assess," to reconnect with the heart of our mission and deduce strategies for accomplishing the commission to make disciples of all the nations. The global church is in a time of transition identified in apostle Paul's teaching as "of the dispensation of the fullness of the times" (Eph. 1:10).

Chapter Two

INTERPRETING TRANSITIONS

Jesus Christ spoke of signs of the end of the ages in his teachings. He warned:

> *Take heed that no one deceives you, For many will come in My name, saying, "I am the Christ," and will deceive many* (Matthew 24:4-5).

Jesus was warning of a time of confusion, and the need for interpretation by those who hold the truth. He warned the world that there would be *"wars and rumors of wars...famines, pestilences, and earthquakes in various places."*[25] But then followers of Christ were to *"See that you are not troubled; for all these things must come to pass, but the end is not yet"*[26]. We were warned of international and civil wars, and also spiritual wars for dominion *"kingdom against kingdom."* The truth of the prophetic hour lies in the hands of the Church[27] ; and we must tell it as a matter of commission to release the earth from the clutches of the forces of darkness. God spoke through an Old Testament prophet revealing an important covenant:

Surely the Lord God does nothing, Unless He reveals His secret to His servants the prophets (Amos 3:7).

Jesus honored the prophetic ministry of John the Baptist:

For I say to you among those born of women there is not a greater prophet than John the Baptist, but he who is least in the Kingdom of God is greater than he (Luke 7:28).

It would be appropriate to remind ourselves briefly of the main crux of John's ministry so that all appreciate the honor he received from the Lord and how that might apply to the Church in our time. John was a both a sign of hope, *"behold I will send you Elijah the prophet"* (Mal. 4:5), and a fulfillment of promised hope, *"For this is he who was spoken of by the prophet Isaiah, saying"* (Matt. 3:3). Jesus referred to John as *"Elijah who is to come"* (Matt. 11:14). The prophet Isaiah spoke of John's forerunning ministry that would prepare the hearts of the people for salvation. John's prophetic ministry would bridge generational gaps necessary for smooth transitions into new spiritual experiences and for continuation of divine mission. Operating in the mantle of Elijah, John's ministry would be used to *"turn the hearts of the fathers to the children, and the hearts of the children to their fathers"* (Mal. 4:6). Generational gaps bring about judgment on a land. The devil loves gaps because his ministry is to create gaps when he is unable to murder a destiny. He creates gaps through trauma to a person or even to land. Trauma separates spirit, body, and soul. In the case of land for instance, trauma attains separation at a point of physical impact from shock such as would occur with bombs or any other form of explosion. The gap or gaps created at the point of physical impact enable demonic forces to set up thrones of iniquity that subsequently serve as "access" points.

John the Baptist identified himself as,

"I am 'The voice of one crying in the wilderness: Make straight the way of the Lord.'" He showed understanding of his own calling when he added, *"as the prophet Isaiah said"* (John 1:23).

Jesus announced His ministry with conviction: *"The Spirit of the Lord is upon Me, for He has anointed Me,"* and He went on to announce His specific ministry (Luke 4:18).

An interesting point to note from John's dialogue with his interrogators in John chapter 1 is that the questions were being asked by the Pharisees. As learned individuals they would have been expected to be conversant with the Book of Isaiah. The Bible records, *"Now those who were sent were from the Pharisees"* (John 1:24). Their lack of spiritual sight was exposed in their ignorance of baptisms. The question asked by the Pharisees paints a picture of present day. Unless the prophets and the Church as a prophetic community rise up to the responsibility of interpreting the Scriptures and unfolding signs of fulfillment, the unsaved will be bound by wrong allegiance. The Pharisees responded to John the Baptist, "Why then do you baptize if you are not the Christ, nor Elijah, nor the Prophet?" (John 1:25). They sought to contain John's ministry within their limited knowledge. *Not* — *I think I can Relate* —

Fresh impetus, interpreted by my humble self as the spirit of Elijah,[28] is to be coveted if the saints are to be equipped as a prophetic army. It is now time to marshal the troops outward into the needy world. The Church can no longer squabble over minor issues but we are to receive the grace of Issachar tribe. We need anointing for clarity, understanding, and knowledge in order to impact our spheres. An uncertain period of confusion is bound to fall upon the Church sooner or later, necessitating assistance of the "sons of God" (Rom. 8:19). The world is fast becoming engulfed with spiritual darkness in fulfillment of prophecy: *"For behold darkness shall cover the earth, and deep darkness the people"* (Isa. 60:2). As such, the Body of Christ has to be prepared to carry the light of Christ, His manifest presence so *"The Gentiles shall come to your light, and kings to the brightness of your rising"* (Isa. 60:3).

Once more, I humbly submit my discernment that the world is in the beginning of the times referred to as *"the dispensation of the fullness of the times"* (Eph. 1:10). The Church needs to seek to understand the prophetic and natural implications of what Paul spoke next: *"He might **gather together in one**[29] all things in Christ, both which* *are in heaven and which are on earth—in Him."* In times of transition interpretative skills provide clarity with hope of escape from the wiles of the devil. These times can be interpreted also as times of "confusion" or "computation" depending on one's spiritual frequency. Unless voids are filled, they remain voids, empty space, that can be filled by any thing or person. Ambiguity creates intellectual void that is replicated in spiritual dynamics. So unless someone or something stands in a gap to bridge voids, spiritual or natural, by giving words to space, confusion takes over.

MIND-SET IS IMPORTANT

The mind-set with which the prophetic church functions in times of transition is crucial to the ultimate victory secured. This is where the interpretative functions of the prophetic gift become vital to bring direction and hope to the Body of Christ. Spiritual climates need to be interpreted with urgency and vigor so that fresh insight for city-taking can be extracted. In times of great revivals of light, revivals of evil tend to challenge the purposes of God as we read in the Book of Acts. Daniel's extreme prophetic ministry developed amid astrologers, diviners, sorcerers, witches, and wizards.[30] The fact is that the global church of Jesus Christ is facing the "Nebucchadnezar" siege, with spiritual exile being the way out of apathy and complacency. In the darkness of Babylon, we must push through into extreme prophetic.

INTERPRETING SPIRITUAL CLIMATES

I live in a suburb of the second largest city in England, also known as the heart of the nation. The Lord spoke to me on September 25, 2004, revealing several things, including the fact that my city carried a "Pergamos" type identity similar to the original Pergamos in the Book of Revelation. The implication being that the Body of Christ in Birmingham would be exposed to the same sin as the church in the original city of Pergamos, also known as "the compromising church." Birmingham had the same spiritual identity as the head nation, Britain, despite being in the heart of England. I was led to a message in a few lines in my Bible beginning, *"To him who overcomes,"* with the Spirit of the Lord amplifying His reward for those who would overcome the strongholds of Pergamos and in each of the other churches Jesus wrote to (Rev. 2–3). I was instantly transformed by this revelation that seemed to infuse new life into my spirit. I was excited by the depth of strategies being revealed for the establishing of His Kingdom in the city of Birmingham, and nations of Britain.

Shortly after my experience, I had a conversation with friends Roger and Sue Mitchell (Passion UK), who incidentally had written some years back about the letters to the angels of the seven churches in their forerunning book.[31] They, in turn, directed me to a new publication by another friend, Martin Scott,[32] whose insight revealed a progression to this profound revelation of city types, modeling after the original churches in the cities the messages addressed (Rev. 2–3). To these well-researched books from respected and experienced apostolic and prophetic voices I add my humble insight by way of a "call." I am in agreement with Martin Scott's claim that "every city has a personality."[33] He went on to confirm the heart of the revelation the Lord was impacting in my spirit with the following:

> ...either the city will shape the church or the church will overcome and shape the city. Increasingly, however, I have come to believe that we can use these letters at yet another level. They can help us discern the personality of a city and understand the strongholds that are typical in that particular type of city.

Sue Mitchell writes: "Like the Lord we must strategize to win a city."[34] She goes on to explain, "Cities...are keys to a region and eventually a nation or a continent." I hold the same opinion as these respected prophets and friends, a fact that will ring through this book as I seek to impart my passion for prophetic repositioning of the Church in this Day of the Lord.

WAR IN PERGAMOS

To the angel of the church in Pergamos, also known as "the compromising church"[35] Jesus wrote: *These things say He who has the*

39

sharp two-edged sword." Jesus is the Word who became flesh and dwelt among men.[36]

Then the complaint: *"But I have a few things against you, because you have there those who hold the doctrine of Balaam, who taught Balak to put a stumbling block before the children of Israel, to eat things sacrificed to idols, and to commit sexual immorality. Thus you also have those who hold the doctrine of the Nicolaitans, which thing I hate"* (Rev. 2:14-15).

INTERPRETING THE DOCTRINE OF THE NICOLAITANS

Can we afford to love what God hates? In 2002 I was privileged to host a dynamic apostle and one of my mentors Dr. Paula Price, author of *The Prophets Dictionary.* Dr. Paula's charge to me as she left Birmingham for Tulsa, Oklahoma, was "study up on the doctrine of the Nicolaitans." I believe I was not spiritually ready to receive the revelation I now share, of strongholds that challenge the light of the Gospel in cities. Birmingham and any other city with the characteristics I will seek to highlight as Pergamos-type would tolerate certain strongholds. Such spiritual climates attract satanic citadels represented by demonic statutes, divination through cloning, or echoing prophetic words. There is control, idolatry, and sexual immorality unless the Church as a body rises up to be as salt and light.

The issue of hierarchical control or doctrine of the Nicolaitans is condoned in the Church by virtue of the compromising character of the original church in the city of Pergamos. God particularly singled out hierarchical control or the doctrine of the Nicolaitans expressing his displeasure as, *"this thing I hate."* The root of the word *Nicolaitans* comes from two Greek words *nikoa* meaning "to conquer or over-come" and *laos* which means "people." Laos is also the word for "laity." Thus Nicolaitans refers to those who prevail or overcome the people or laity. Jesus hates any attempt to overcome his people. He died to set us free and so He pronounced reward for those who prevailed to overcome the strongholds in their cities. It is interesting to note that the church in Ephesus was commended for hating the deeds

40

of Nicolaitans. Jesus found comrades in Ephesus who hated *"the deeds of the Nicolaitans, which I also hate"* (Rev. 2:6).

After discovering through prayer and revelation that Nigeria stood on the same timeline on God's prophetic clock as Britain, I began studying the capital city, Abuja, in the heart of Nigeria for similarities with Birmingham. The church in Nigeria and Abuja appeared to reveal strong Nicolaitan tendencies. In this case the Nicolaitans stronghold was strengthened through "false respect," a cultural weakness that made room for spiritual slavery. The culture of respect of elders left the church vulnerable and perpetuated the deeds of the Nicolaitans: overcoming the people. Both nations and cities exhibited "physical characteristics"[37] of original Pergamos.

Sue Mitchell, a good friend and respected prophet, inspired me to pray for further revelation on a spiritually safe place, a Smyrna type in our city. I subsequently recognized Yardley Wood as one Smyrna type, a place receptive to prophetic activities.

UNMASKING THE SPIRIT OF DEATH *Rome - the Pope -*

An important spiritual dynamic of Pergamos worth more than a mention is the connection with the spirit of death. The original Pergamos was identified as *"where Satan's throne is."* It was also a place of sacrificial death as revealed in the mention of Antipas as *"My faithful martyr who was killed among you, where Satan dwells"* (Rev. 2:13). Jesus revealed through His letter to the angel of Pergamos an important weapon for the saints in cities and nations whose present spiritual climate manifests identical strongholds as the original Pergamos. It is interesting that in a place where satan's throne dwells, considering satan is the spirit of death, whose agenda is to steal, kill and destroy[38], a faithful servant gave his life to defeat the spirit of death.

Martyrdom of Antipas is seen as spiritual leverage for the church in cities with Pergamos spiritual climates to defeat the fear element used by the enemy to bring premature death to divine missions. The Lord spoke to me recently as I battled the same spirit. Jesus could have gone to glory like Enoch,[39] a chariot of fire could have come for him like Elijah,[40] or he could have fallen asleep like Stephen,[41] after all he is the Son of God. But He revealed that He had to confront and defeat "death" by dying at the Cross.[42] He revealed that since "death" would be the end-time principality warring against us, the Church,[43] He had to confront death once and for all. The antichrist is masked as death, and the Bible recognizes him as *"the man of sin"* and the *"son of perdition"* (see 2 Thess. 2:3). He is the principality behind the lawlessness of our time, a deceiver.[44] The spirit of the antichrist is the spirits that boast in their own destruction,[45] the lying spirit who denies Christ's supremacy.[46] The antichrist spirits are behind unrighteous laws promulgated in many nations of the West. The Bible warned, *"It is the last hour; and as you have heard that the Antichrist is coming, even now many antichrists have come, by which we know that it is the last hour"* (1 John 2:18).

Environments with physical manifestations of Pergamos strongholds are receptive to demonic statutes and other symbols of idolatry. It would be no surprise to find attitudes of control, divination, and tendency to clone ministry gifts in churches as part of the Balaamic stronghold. The war of the churches in such climates would be fierce, with the spirit of death as the main enemy. This spirit seeks to cut short the hope and expectation of the righteous contrary to the Word of God (Prov. 23:18). The intended agenda of this principality is to attack the faith foundation of believers in Christ. With the best of intentions, believers may find themselves giving in to compromise due to pressure from negativity rife in this type of spiritual climate.[47]

A major implication of the Pergamos identity of cities is transported through the vehicle of freemasonry. For instance, freemasonry was imported and received by the city of Birmingham through demonic spiritual pathways. Natural trade pathways create spiritual access into lives and environments. The original spiritual pathways in my city now serve as freeways to forces of darkness. Foundations of education, medicine, and other fields of excellence in our city, laid partly by Masonic economic influence, are actually access points to demonic activities. A modern-day coalition of evil now wages intense spiritual warfare against Kingdom initiatives, with the Church largely asleep. It is important to note that "church" is no threat to demonic activities in a Pergamos-type city or nation. But the devil dreads the establishing of the Kingdom of God in our time through people who know their God, people who *"shall be strong and carry out great exploits"*[48] for Christ.

PASSING THROUGH THE VALLEY OF THE SHADOW OF DEATH

The Spirit of the Lord also revealed that in a Pergamos-type spiritual climate, times of *transition* could be misinterpreted as spiritual *death.* Transition means *"passing or change from one place, state, condition to another."* Death means *"the fact or state of being dead, the ending of life, the destruction or permanent cessation of something (was the death of our hopes)."*[49] Unless believers responsibly interpret their experiences while transitioning through *"the valley of the shadow of death,"*[50] vacuums may be created. The devil then enforces his death sentences *"to steal, and to kill, and to destroy"*[51] in vacuums. God-ordained purposes carry the breath of God[52] and are thus sustained through difficult times.[53]

In my experience as a Christian leader interacting at all levels, I find that when ministries or individual believers are transitioning from one stage of spiritual development to another, the greatest threat comes from the "spirit of death." These vision-destroying spirits lurk in the background hoping to set up thrones and altars of deception in vacuums created where the people lack understanding of their journey.[54] Death gives off one signal, "extinction," whereas transition offers "hope" for the future.

> But we all, with unveiled face, beholding as in a mirror the glory of the Lord, are being transformed into the same image from glory to glory, just as by the Spirit of the Lord (2 Corinthians 3:18).

God's plans for his children are for fruitfulness and continuity, to take us from one level of brilliance to another. Unless the interpretative function of the prophetic gift is actively employed, many Kingdom objectives may be buried prematurely or at best re-named even by the most anointed of God. The call for cross bearers or humble vessels may be read as a call for funeral undertakers. The devil attacks through subtle ploys of evil, and wages his war of deception against the saints. His objective is to cause a derailing of God's intended purposes through spiritual abortion or miscarriage. The devil longs to "destroy" original identities through which Kingdom visions are established as terrors to the enemy in Pergamos-type cities and nations—*"where Satan's throne is"* (Rev. 2:13).

OVERCOMING IN PERGAMOS

To overcome the devil in a satanic domain necessitates a stubborn resolve to function in the resurrection power of Christ. This is a mind-set of the supernatural life and power.[55] Apostle Paul warned the church in Corinth: *"For the kingdom of God is not in word but in power"* (1 Cor. 4:20). To overcome the principalities of spiritual Pergamos the Church needs to be tenacious,[56] and passionate[57] in expressing the Kingdom of God within each believer.[58] Jesus came to give life and to give life in abundance.[59] Followers of Christ are to choose to live in abundant life, accomplishing extraordinary exploits in everyday life. This mind-set is opposed to the spirits of death that are attracted to spiritual Pergamos. Living in abundant life necessitates functioning in positivity, proactivity, and productivity.

IDENTIFYING GOD'S LAUNCHING PADS FOR COUNTER ATTACKS

Smyrna-type climates exhibit physical characteristics of tribulation and poverty, able to endure slandering. The spiritual climate I describe as Smyrna-type is easily identified as being conducive to ministries with dogged, long-lasting qualities necessary to frustrate the controlling and seducing spirits of Pergamos. Martin Scott sees Smyrna-type climates as "places of deliverance." I agree with the notion of deliverance amid darkness.[60] Jesus introduced himself to the angel of the church in Smyrna as *"the First and the Last, who was dead, and came to life"* (Rev. 2:8). As I pondered over these words, the Lord began to reveal that the key to Pergamos' redemption lays in Smyrna. Such places should be considered possible host areas for Kingdom visions established to function in the opposite spirit of "church mind-set." The saints of Smyrna understood spiritual gaps, as they were greeted by Jesus in the character He revealed to each city church. To Smyrna He is, *"The First and the Last, who was dead and came to life,"*[61] and to Pergamos, *"He who has the sharp two-edged sword."*[62] The saints in Smyrna could draw strength from Christ's own sufferings while the saints in Pergamos must seek strength and stability from the truth of His Gospel, the Word of God (Heb. 4:12).

Smyrna is relevant for breaking through the barriers of Pergamos because of the bridge-building and gap-filling gifts revealed in the letter to the church in Smyrna. This church identifies with the threats from confusion in places where gaps in understanding of spiritual dynamics are allowed. Jesus wrote, *"Indeed the devil is about to throw some of you into prison, that you may be tested, and you will have tribulation ten days"* (Rev. 2:10). The church in Smyrna possesses the overcoming quality of sacrificial living that negates the plans of the spirit of death. To them Jesus wrote, *"Be faithful until death, and I will give you the crown of life"* (Rev. 2:10). He goes on to reveal the reward for overcomers: *"He who overcomes shall not be hurt by the second death"* (Rev. 2:11). Could individual believers in Christ Jesus bear in their natural qualities the same characteristics singled out by Jesus in His letters to the seven churches of the Book of Revelation?

RENAMING KINGDOM VISIONS: ANOTHER FORM OF DEATH

The spirits at work in Pergamos operate in different identities but ultimately their agenda is simply to kill Kingdom visions. As already mentioned, if the devil is not successful in exterminating the original name with which a God-ordained vision is called forth, he subtly suggests renaming—a comfortable alternative. Renaming a God-named initiative may have the same implication or connotation as pronouncing death. I know this from my culture as an Ibo from Southern Nigeria where names reveal the identity of the bearer. Families pray for eight days before pronouncing destiny through naming. It is common practice in Ibo custom to have male members of a family name a child. One of the privileges God gave Adam before the fall was the power to name: *"And whatever Adam called each living creature, that was its name"* (Gen. 2:19). To an Ibo, life is in the name given—another way of saying, "life is in the name given to a child." The Ibo believe a person's future is determined by the name given, hence most names begin or end with "Chi" or "Chu" meaning God Almighty. Such is the importance of names that a person's life is to be seen as a prophetic fulfillment of their name. So, like Jabez,[63] believers whose ancestors worshiped idols renounced certain names after conversion, reflecting their new life as "born again." Many go as far as a legal name change or public declaration in the newspaper. This practice is still common in Nigeria, a nation with one of the largest populations of born-again Christians in the world.

I fail to see how the Lord can call believers to establish Kingdom visions with an identity and then turn around to ask for that identity to be buried. Projects can be named according to phases of development, but a vision shifts from the casting stage into processes that lead to fulfillment (Num. 23:19). This pattern is seen in the ministry of Jesus Christ, our Lord (Luke 4:18). He did not work outside of the vision he announced: *"The Spirit of the Lord is upon Me,"* but it multiplied in the hands of the disciples. The Pharisees and Sadducees, on the other hand, with distorted spiritual sight renamed their agenda of "death" through tricky questioning, blackmail, and so forth. Every time they tried to catch Jesus, their plot was launched in a new name including "lying, deceit, accusation, and finally death by nailing." The Kingdom mind-set understands "death by nailing"—our hope of glory. It is therefore important for the Church to interpret transitions for natural and spiritual survival. Only then can the Church deploy all her troops to help the secular world interpret natural changes. There is a need to seek deeper insight into Scriptures that shed light to our present corporate journey. When spiritual seeds fall to the ground and die, they ought to bring forth a harvest of life.[64] Such seeds are to multiply life.

INTERPRETING DOCTRINE OF BALAAM

The devil does not possess power or authority to curse anything or anyone the Lord has blessed.[65] Aware of his fate in these last days,[66] the devil wields his evil rod of deception the same old weapon with which Eve was conned in the Garden of Eden.[67] The devil manipulates believers into pronouncing death sentences on God's preordained missions.[68] I remember facing severe spiritual warfare during 2005 as the devil strategically engineered an attempt to intimidate me into pronouncing death on an international prayer ministry I had the privilege of birthing in 1995. When his efforts were frustrated, he changed tactics, this time suggesting a new name for the ministry. I was led by the Spirit of the Lord to resist a name change at the time because I recognized the demon I was dealing with to be the spirit of death. We knew the ministry was in a time of transition and also that a new name had been given by which the vision was to continue into multiplication. The aim of the spirit of death was to rename the ministry at a time of transition, thereby creating confusion for those who would carry the vision forward.

Death and life are in the power of the tongue, and those who love it will eat its fruit (Proverbs 18:21).

The devil deceives the Church through familiar spirits that understand spiritual weaknesses and prevalent sin in an area. In our case the devil knew our city to be a place of burial of Kingdom vision, so at the first attempt he offered a coffin which I promptly rejected. These evil spirits at work in Pergamos-type cities are strengthened by the state of the hearts they choose to war with. They act on previously seduced and compromised hearts of God's people who, in competition with one another, desire "death" for competing ministries. So, unrighteousness in the heart opens the door for the devil to strike with the intent to destroy (John 10:10).

The devil understands Scripture; he knows the tongue holds the power of death and life (Prov. 18:21). According to the Word of God whichever choice a person is bound to produces fruit that must be eaten, "*And those who love it will eat its fruit.*" The fruit of negative speech leads to death or loss of some kind. Equally, the devil knows the prophetic church has been endowed with the power of God's creative word: "*You will also declare a thing, and it shall be established for you*" (Job 22:28). The power of positive speech produces renewal and revival. Since the devil cannot kill what the Lord has called forth and named, he deceives the only created beings with the authority to establish and disestablish to speak negatively. Balak hired Balaam with the commission: "*Please come at once, curse this people for me, for they are too mighty for me*" (Num. 22:6). But the Lord replaced any curses with blessing so Balaam questioned: "*How shall I curse whom God has not cursed? And how shall I denounce whom the Lord has not denounced?*" (Num. 23:8). Blessing releases divine favor with which the Church wins the enemy in Pergamos climates. By offering unrighteous counsel, Balaam led Israel astray into sexual immorality,[69] with the elders of Israel also compromising (Num. 31:16). These tendencies must be avoided by the church in spiritual Pergamos.

The doctrine of Balaam is rooted in greed and false hope. With existing compromise in the foundation of believers' hearts the enemy captivates the heart into wrongdoing or outright idolatry. Roger and Sue Mitchell touch on the implication of greed in the foundation of our hearts. In their opinion, "Satanic strongholds build up from the starting point of individual sin and end in corporate demonization"[70] as was the case with Judas Iscariot. Unless the heart is cleared of residing unrighteousness, the devil will continue challenging the destinies of believers.

FAMILIAR SPIRITS ARE DEMONIC AGENTS

The devil operates in Pergamos spiritual climates through "familiar spirits." Once an initial sin creates an entry point for the enemy to strike at a believer, such openings remain porous until repentance. Identificational repentance of past and existing sin is able to shut the door in the face of familiar spirits.[71] Continual sin eventually constitutes an invitation for the devil to take control of the hearts and minds[72] of God's people. Familiar spirits are unintelligent demonic beings that attack on the back of an initial attack following a pathway already created through past sin. Familiar spirits are attracted to the Pergamos spiritual climate, feeding on Balaamite doctrine or divination. Familiar spirits are deployed and used to accuse the same compromising traits the devil encourages in seduced believers. The devil is no friend to a child of God. We are warned in the Bible: *"The heart is deceitful above all things, and desperately wicked; Who can know it?"* (Jer. 17:9). If spiritual activities in a Pergamos-type city, as in my case study, are carefully tracked, the reality of repeated spiritual attacks will be revealed through patterns and sequences of such attacks. The anointing of Issachar enables interpretation of demonic activities that challenge the Kingdom of God in an area. The devil is not creative, he only repeats activities in lives and places he has had a foothold in the past.

Through my observation over a number of years of spiritual activities in the two cities mentioned, I have drawn a conclusion that the devil operates in a *two-year cycle* of death. This cycle can only be broken by a united force in right standing with the Lord. In two-year cycles the devil unleashes death attacks against the church where in some cases pastors of spirit-filled churches are changed in cycles. Changes to strategic positioning of spiritual authority come masked in bureaucratic language, and appear innocent. However, it is important for movement at certain levels of spiritual authority in strategic cities to be interpreted, especially where a clear pattern is visible. The intention of the enemy is usually to achieve death or cause premature burial of any life or ministry seeking to see the establishment of God's Kingdom.

Since Pergamos-type cities are also known as *establishing* cities, it makes sense for the devil to resist the redemptive gift of the area. Attempts to establish roots or long-lasting initiatives or relationships are aggressively challenged in the same cycle. My team and I have observed the traits enumerated for years and have put in place suggested safeguards. I have found purity of heart to be the safest human weapon while the blood of Jesus remains the dread of the enemies of spiritual Pergamos. These cities remain vulnerable to the foundational issues

49

similar to ones highlighted by Jesus as offensive in His letter to the angel of Pergamos. The existence in the Church of the doctrines of the Nicolaitans and Balaam remain an offense to our Lord. These deeds constitute a challenge to the establishing of God's Kingdom.

New paradigm calls for right speech speaking life into God-breathed initiatives to destroy the works of the devil: *"For this purpose the Son of God was manifested, that He might destroy the works of the devil"* (1 John 3:8). Believers in Christ are the only hope the unsaved have for salvation (Rom. 8:19). If God-ordained initiatives are killed by the enemy then he succeeds in controlling the lives of *"the sons of disobedience"* (Eph. 2:2).

CULTURE COMES INTO PLAY

There is also a cultural dynamic to spiritual activities in a Pergamos-type city or nation as indeed anywhere else.[73] The historical Pergamos mentioned in the Book of Revelation was a Roman citadel, the official seat of the Roman government. A 200-foot-high altar to Zeus, the Greek god, stood in her domain. Pergamos was the center of the worship of Aesclepius, the god of healing, whose symbol was a serpent. The symbol of the modern-day medical profession is a rod and snake. Although not bearing any direct relationship with the sign of Aesclepius, it is important to bear in mind the fact that the enemy perverts good gifts. Martin Scott pointed out in his book that, "Hospitals and, in particular medical research, will prosper in these cities."[74]

In seeking to inspire and provoke the prophetic community to discern more accurately and interpret signs around our world, my intention is not to be out of balance with the information I place before you. However, the responsibility of those who serve in the fivefold function of prophet should go beyond declaring information. The same call of the Spirit to John to ascend into a higher place of revelation is relevant today.[75] New strategies are needed to free the souls of young people bound by drugs, alcohol, and sex. Perverted foundations of socializing serve as launching pads to effect demonic assignments worked in cycles, patterns, and sequences. As stewards of God's manifest grace[76] and watchmen over cities and nations, believers are required to persevere in frustrating the devil's rod: *"Lest the righteous reach out their hands to iniquity"* (Ps. 125:3).

The saints in natural Pergamos were chastised for holding onto Balaamite doctrine. Israel succumbed to Balaam's unscrupulous counsel with the effect that their men were contaminated by Moabite women (Num. 25). Every believer in Christ Jesus is endowed with supernatural inner will, conviction, and faith necessary to worship the Lord in spirit and truth.[77] Christian leaders must heed the urgent call from heaven to equip the saints for the work of the ministry.[78] Impartation of prophetic grace and activation of other supernatural gifts would see the corporate Body of Christ in a city becoming more decisive, effective, and less suspicious of one another.

POWER OF POSITIVE SPEECH

Words are powerful, carrying creative abilities of God, especially when ensuing from believers in Jesus Christ. Any words that undermine the divine will of God for a believer's life should be rejected outright, especially when spoken in spiritual climates that welcome negativity. The devil uses such words to unleash the spirit of death in a well-organized pattern operated through demonic cycles.

With profound responsibilities to affect communities with the resurrection power, believers will hinder their own purposes by speaking negatively. The Bible reminds: *"Faith by itself, if it does not have works, is dead."*[79] Any mind-set short of radical belief will encourage the sort of compromise Pergamos was chastized for. It is the responsibility of the prophetic community to teach believers to speak words that line up with the holy Word of God. Unless we incubate life within the chambers of our mouths, hope cannot be transmitted through the Body of Christ. Believers who speak negatively in spiritual Pergamos may find themselves in partnership with the devil to curse God's plans and purposes (Matt. 28:19). The intentions may be pure and innocent, but negative speech could still empower the spirit of death in Pergamos climates. The devil does not make excuses for negativity spoken innocently. He is the accuser of the brethren (Rev. 12:10). Ignorance of the law is not an acceptable defense in English law. So a murderer cannot claim immunity from the law by simply claiming, "I forgot that it is wrong to kill a person." The Bible makes clear the power of agreement.[80]

TIMELINES HELP US INTERPRET SPIRITUAL MATTERS

I have a keen interest in understanding God's timeline but more particularly, where nations stand on His timeline. Clarity of timelines will help the Church function more effectively as a "watchman,"[81] and be able to warn more accurately. Spiritual activities mirror-image themselves down timelines. I would like to defer once more to the two nations of interest, Britain and Nigeria, identified in my study as occupiers of the same spiritual timeline. The devil thrives on perceived cultural weaknesses of nations and cities to attack the church in such places. So, in a culture of civility for instance, the devil deceives the church through *false humility*. Believers receive negative pronouncements over their lives, unaware of future implications of such words. The deceiver tricks people into entering verbal agreements that empower demonic forces that oppose any "Kingdom" vision. Taking advantage of a culture of civility that imposes polite acceptance of negativity, the devil unleashes death spirits against the church.

Similarly a culture with a custom of respect of elders is attacked through church leadership. The devil manipulates the hearts of believers through the age or hierarchy card. The culture battle in such a nation attracts more of the Nicolaitans, hierarchical control issues, *another form of false humility*. Agreements are covenants which need not be entered into as a matter of cultural allegiance. Any agreements or covenants not emanating from sincere heart alignments may be interpreted as a form of false humility. The principalities at work in Pergamos-type spiritual climates war against heart agreements. The antichrist contends destinies from the hearts of nations. The devil exploits cultural weaknesses, subtly leading believers into compromise through fear and false humility. The Church is at war with the same devil dressed in different national costumes. The messages to the angels of the churches in the Book of Revelation hold the key to the Church's breakthrough.

An extension of the concept of "death or life" in Pergamos" leads me to conclude that "death" attacks the church in Pergamos through familiar routes of *negative speech, competition, rivalry, control, and false hope.* The doctrine of Balaam fosters false hope. Balak hired Balaam to curse the advancing Israelites who were on their way to the Promised Land. Both nations of my study are praying nations making Pergamos a place of quality soldiers of the Lord identified as *"to him who overcomes"* (Rev. 2:17). To break through, believers in Christ in such cities and nations must operate in the opposite spirit of divination, control, idolatry, manipulation, cloning, and sins of the mouth.

During October 2003, the Lord spoke to my heart to reveal a call to the realm of martyrdom (Rev. 12:11). He defined modern-day martyrdom as "sufferings" and persecutions that would be likened to death (1 Pet. 4:12-14). The experience I was made to see with the eyes of my spirit was described as "being martyred by the tongue." The likeness of death revealed would come from slandering, libel, gossip, and all manner of tongue lashing. With hindsight and benefit of revelation, individuals may carry a Smyrna identity and destiny with resolve of apostle Paul who said, *"For I am already being poured out as a drink offering"* (2 Tim. 4:6). The Lord revealed those who overcome in Smyrna will not fear the second death. Those who overcome are, in our time, people who refuse to compromise but instead are willing to face the consequences of bearing witness for Christ. Truth will be rare in the last days and overcomers would be victimized for speaking truth (Acts 7:59-60). Modern-day martyrs would be victims of sins of the tongue, facing false accusations, but their vindication would come from the Lord (Isa. 54:17). So, in Pergamos-type spiritual climates believers would be seduced by the devil to undermine one another through speech. The Body of Christ in such climates prevail through violent praise,[82] worship,[83] and generosity of spirit.[84] What the devil seeks to pervert by killing names of Kingdom visions named by God is a promise to those who remain faithful in Pergamos: *"And I will give him a white stone, and on the stone a new name written which no one knows except him who receives it"* (Rev. 2:17). It is said that juries voted for acquittal by casting a white stone in an urn. Special stones were also given as reward to winners in some games. The blood of Jesus has acquitted us as believers in His grace. The new name received in the imputed character of God is known only by a saint who remains faithful to overcome in Pergamos, an establishing city.

AWAKEN THE COMPROMISING CHURCH

And do this, knowing the time, that now it is high time to awake out of sleep; for now our salvation is nearer than when we first believed (Romans 13:11).

There is a call for "Amos-type" prophetic ministries with prophets bearing burdens of God's complaints against the nations. We are in a time of major spiritual upheavals and shifts affecting natural life. The displeasure of God with unrighteousness and rebellious nations and peoples calls for more Amos-type prophets. Incidentally, the name Amos means "burden bearer." Prophets are to boldly prepare the Church to march onward to the real world—as we are commissioned to do. We no longer need professionalism; we simply need a prophetic revolution. The role of prophets in this season is to condition the spiritual ears of the Church to discern and to hear truth. Amos' humility should be encouragement for those who feel unqualified to hear the Lord. Amos testified:

> I was no prophet,
> Nor was I a son of a prophet,
> But I was a sheepbreeder,
> And a tender of sycamore fruit.
> Then the Lord spoke to me as I followed the flock,
> And the Lord said to me,
> 'Go, prophesy to My people Israel' (Amos 7:14-15).

SETTING THE PACE

We need to call for bold expressions of the multidimensional wisdom of God through prophetic pastors, teachers, and evangelists. Apostles and prophets need to set God's people solid in present truth, helping defeat the enemies of our time. In a Pergamos-type city, the prophetic church is to set spiritual pace by sincerely serving the purposes of God with conviction, and passion. Hence I agree with Martin Scott's summation that, "either the city will shape the church or the church will overcome and shape the city."[85]

Chapter Three

·•· ≅◊≅ ·•·

TIME TO CROSS OVER

The mind-set necessary in times of transitions is captured in the instruction given to the Israelites before the Jordan River crossing.[86] At such times, we must be willing to follow the presence of God with childlike innocence. The blood of Jesus bridged every gap and has given the Body of Christ a new route of inheritance (see Eph. 3:12). But so long as the Church continues to drive her own agenda on every level then the power of the Cross is denied us. There is a fresh call to the Church to cross over from mundane living to supernatural manifestations of Kingdom attributes. Apostle Paul made this truth known to the Corinthian church when he said: *"For the message of the cross is foolishness to those who are perishing, but to us who are being saved it is the power of God"* (1 Cor. 1:18).

COMMUNICATION IS IMPORTANT

To combat the lies of satan spoken through some of the false, deceiving doctrines the world is being subjected to, the prophetic church needs to fill existing gaps in communication. As discussed in the previous chapter, unless transitions are interpreted and communicated clearly the

Church may suffer unnecessary loss. Transition should be understood as passage to greater emphasis of God's power on the earth.

Jesus served the purpose of God with humility (see John 3:16). The authority He had from his Father was transferred to His disciples (see Matt. 28:18). He left no gaps in the clarity with which vision-continuation was communicated to the disciples just before His resurrection, *"Go therefore and make disciples of all the nations, baptizing them in the name of the Father and of the Son and of the Holy Spirit"* (Matt. 28:19). The disciples were not left in the dark concerning the source of power to pursue the next level of vision, nor did they have to grovel before receiving empowerment. The instructions for fulfillment of prophetic destiny were clear and simple: *"Tarry in the city of Jerusalem until you are endued with power from on high"* (Luke 24:49); *"You shall receive power when the Holy Spirit has come upon you"* (Acts 1:8).

The purpose of vision is fulfilled through effective communication. The essence of vision is that those who pursue it will take it to another level. Hence God spoke to Habakkuk to transcribe the vision so that those who fulfill it can connect with its heart at the appointed time (see Hab. 2:3). To run the path of vision, it needs to be made clear. Worship and prayer birthed the purpose of God on earth through 120 disciples who gathered in the upper room (see Acts 1). When observers misunderstood the disciples as drunk, Peter stood in the gap to interpret the manifestations of the Spirit's power.[87] Peter did not take advantage of the novelty of tongues to promote himself. He could have organized "come let us tell you how it all happened" conferences—but he didn't.

COMMUNICATING VISION IN TIMES OF TRANSITION

Vision has to be communicated clearly, especially in times of transition, in order to maintain continuity of purpose. The Lord spoke a nugget into my heart recently that is probably obvious to many other believers. He spoke specifically to times of transition, revealing that, *"It takes vision to make a people and it takes people to make a vision."* He was not judging present achievements, but on the contrary, seeks to envision our future. Vision is constantly unfolding, hence revelation remains progressive. Our destiny as prophetic vessels is rooted in the Word of God which is settled in Heaven, and is a closed book. However the outworking of destiny unfolds as we move through the processes of life. The Lord was directly addressing seasons commonly described as "next level" in Christian charismatic experience. The seasons birth new facets of our unfolding divine purpose. The Lord was fulfilling His role as Prophet in my life by infusing me with present truth.

Two stages of prophetic development are necessary for a "next level" movement. The Lord simply spoke into my heart, *"It takes vision to make a people, and it takes people to make a vision."* I went through a process of analyzing this insight, arriving at the conclusion that my hearing was referring to an important part of the Issachar Mandate. It is now time for the Church to equip the prophetic saints for the work of the ministry. The second part of the nugget revealed the part equipped believers would play in the corporate commission of the Church. The Issachar Mandate is a call to the prophetic saints to embark on radical journeys of obedience to be salt and light in our communities (see Matt. 5:13-14). The time has come for prophetic engagement with our world; this is the heartcry of the Issachar Mandate.

It Takes Vision To Make a People

The importance of mind positioning or state of mind of believers in gathered church assemblies is fundamental to achieving the great commission. Unless believers are envisioned in a time of transition the tendency is to have members functioning in the mind-set of an old dispensation. Functionality and vision work hand in hand. An individual member's state of mind will determine the quality of corporate spiritual output. A radical prophetic army must be raised to interpret the present day confusion across the generations. The greatest demand on the prophetic gift at present is as a tool for unlocking divine mysteries with the hope of extracting strategies. Spiritual gifts were given to the Church by the Holy Spirit to be manifested for the profit of all. The impact of prophecy and other gifts on the early church is to be taken as inspiration for greater manifestation of supernatural power in our time. With the tsunami disaster in Asia, hurricanes in the U.S.A., and wars in Africa, many questions are being directed at God. The Church remains the representative of Christ on earth with the anointing to predict and perceive the mind of Christ. Some questions being raised are for the Church to answer while some are entrusted to the hands of God.

Unless the minds of believers are rightly positioned through teaching to receive present day truth, the possibilities open to the Body of Christ to reach the lost will be wasted.[88] The Church must equip and release the entire army of God for the global harvest of souls. The role of the prophetic church has changed while some within the Body of Christ still argue over minor issues of theological excesses. At this first stage of prophetic development, the gathered Church must equip the saints for the work of the ministry. It takes vision to make a people.

IT TAKES PEOPLE TO MAKE A VISION

An important part of purpose fulfillment rests upon people envisioning. The second stage of the two stage prophetic development process the Lord revealed to me for Kingdom advancement would see members of congregations actively involved. With the members of a gathered church assembly now envisioned with purpose, the leaders will find a more focused involvement. Past mind-set has paid attention to body positioning with pastors concerned with the number of members on the books. Training and equipping strategies reflected loyalty of members to the vision of the church. Jesus Christ is coming back for His Bride, the prophetic church—how ready is she?

With members equipped and envisioned for practical ministry, the Church should become more effective. Evangelism targets will be achievable only when members are infused with vision. The minds of members should be strategically positioned to embrace the corporate mandate of the Body of Christ (see Matt. 28:19; Mark 16:15). As previously mentioned, a major function of the prophetic grace is to interpret the times. This ability was recognized and commended in the tribe of Issachar, *"who had understanding of the times, to know what Israel ought to do"* (1 Chron. 12:32). Instead of confining their unusual gift to tribal matters, the children of Issachar served Israel in general. Issacharites were part of David's chosen warring men who fought to see the plans of God established by installing God's elected leadership in Israel. Incidentally, the tribe of Issachar was part of Deborah's prophetic army who ousted Sisera.[89]

The prophetic Bride of Christ is being called to change her garments at this time.[90] There are great needs in our societies for which the prophetic church remains the only body endowed with supernatural ability to bring transformation to previously dark areas.[91] The Church is to be salt, and is to be light in the world. Prophecy as a spiritual gift must mature beyond oral expression or body shivers to regain strategic, impacting power status that helped turn the world upside down in times past.[92] There is a call to the prophetic church to transition into her apostolic destiny to be that house of revealing glory of God. It is my hope that through the chapters of this book the voice of believers calling to the Church to prepare the way of the Lord can be heard. The church has entered an age of prophetic revolution, with new expressions of the prophetic coming through from radical children and youths. The challenge is to discern with distinction, and to serve the heart of Christ in the world He came and died for.

Chapter Four

LIFE IN THE SPIRIT

Aim: To emphasize the inherent abilities of believers to function in supernatural abilities. Life in the Spirit offers a fresh look at the advantages to the world of an envisioned and engaged prophetic army.

God is Spirit, and those who worship Him must worship in spirit and truth (John 4:24).

Life in the Spirit refers to the supernatural dimension of ministry the Church must now conduct as a matter of course.[93] To expect less of those Jesus laid down His life for would be ludicrous. God's power was clearly seen through apostle Paul's ministry, confirming the power in the corporate mantle received by the disciples was not exhausted in their time. As a matter of fact Paul may be seen as an extension of that power, as he was not one of the original 12 apostles.

GOD'S PLAN FOR YOU

Until the return of Christ, the supernatural realm—where the impossible is not only conceivable but achievable—must be lived out as a lifestyle through His believers. Complacency only sets in when the tangible power of God is missing from our lives. Without the Lord's accompanying power the Church stands no chance of accomplishing her divine mission. God's heart is to vindicate His people with His manifest presence and power to confirm the sharing of His Word.[94]

To function in fulfilled promises as a matter of lifestyle is to be received as a dimension of ministry every child of God needs now to covet.[95] Spiritual gifts enable us to function in an enhanced mind-set of the supernatural. The message of this book is to be heard and read as a wake-up call to the army of God. My message is being spoken in time to a people with amazing destiny, but who for some reason have been awaiting a "Samuel" with a horn of oil to anoint their heads.

The global Body of Christ will need to awaken out of slumber to accomplish the corporate destiny for which Christ died. Spiritual climates of many nations at present reveal a "Mount Carmel"-type moment. It would appear, especially for Europe, that the Body of Christ is faced with a literal head-on collision with the 450 prophets of Baal. The Christian faith is being challenged at various levels through government policies and sympathies. Lobby groups not satisfied with ridiculing our faith attempt to enlarge their tentacles at the expense of Christianity. Propagators of humanism operating under the guise of democracy drive antichrist agendas with ignominy. How does the Church deal with or respond to these spiritual challenges of our present day? This is the call of the Issachar Mandate—prophetic engagement.

PASSION FOR THE SUPERNATURAL

Passion for Christ is a prerequisite to supernatural living. We must be consumed with passion to do His will, humbly reaching out for the assurance of His Spirit. Jesus was forthright about His desire to do the will of His Father. As His followers, and those who must function in the Issachar grace, our lives should be modeled after our Lord's. We must burn with passion to do the will of Christ, to preach the Gospel of the Kingdom to every creature. The Church is being called in this hour to manifest the glory of God in practical ways,[96] to worship the

Lord with our lives and with our substance. A believer who sets out to seek spiritual gifts rather than the giver of gifts is bound to live without the accrediting power of the Holy Spirit. Such persons will reap the seeds of their unrighteous motivation.[97] A radical mind shift requires every believing child of God to now desire supernatural manifestations of Christ through their lives and ministries. A parallel shift in the heavens reveals aggressive wars against the purposes of God not only for the Church but also for the world we have been commissioned to save. To operate in the right spiritual balances the Church needs to sort out in-house issues such as mind-set of the believers in Christ Jesus.

A benefactor of a will has legal rights conferred by the will. Any other persons not named in a will making claims under the will would have to go through the legal processes to establish reasons for claiming in the first place. Christians are heirs and heiresses of divine inheritance in the blood of Jesus. Spiritual gifts are embodiments and benefits of the new status gained in the blood of Jesus. They have been given to enable believers to accomplish the mission of soul winning. God is not with self-seeking ministries. Their prayers are allowed to fall to the ground unanswered (see 1 Sam. 3:19). Jesus' disciples received spiritual authority to accomplish a divinely-ordained mission that would otherwise have been humanly challenging. Our challenge as believers in Christ today is to access divine authority as a matter of lifestyle, to exercise as a matter of mission the same if not greater power of God as the early church experienced.

AND THERE WAS JOY IN THE CITY

Spiritual gifts are not borne out of natural abilities or human charisma but have been given by the divine grace of the Spirit of God. The apostles enjoyed tremendous power as several testimonies in the Book of Acts confirm. We are now mandated to progress that mantle of power. A power plant is of no use to humans if it never generates enough energy to be transmitted and distributed as electricity for human comfort. Apart from the apostles, the entire church of the early age was sustained in the supernatural dimension of ministry by the sheer determination to obey the commission to preach the Gospel. In one account of Philip's ministry in Samaria, the power of God was undeniably present as he preached. The Bible records:

> *And the multitudes with one accord heeded the things spoken by Philip, hearing and seeing the miracles which he did For unclean spirits, crying with a loud voice, came out of many who were possessed; and many who were paralyzed and lame were healed; And there was great joy in that city* (Acts 8:6-8).

Every culture, religion, or tradition understands the language of supernatural power. We read of ceaseless visits of celebrities such as the late Princess Diana to psychics, spiritists, and other new age practitioners in search of succor. Many in our societies are searching for answers in attempts to fill voids created by confusion from mixed sounds of our world. Sadly, the Church continues to fail in her role as interpreter and translator. In the face of aggression from often persistent lobbyists, the Church cuts a picture of a weakened, divided body. Secular interests keenly observe trends as one denomination contradicts the other on morality issues such as gay marriages and abortion.

MIRACLES, SIGNS, AND WONDERS ARE NEEDED

The account of Philip's ministry should motivate ministries wishing to impact cities and nations. The Bible records: *"and there was great joy in that city."* Homeless, drug-sick youths, have become familiar eyesores in many Western cities in the 21st century. Human expectation has not changed or diminished since Philip's time. Many city mayors today would wish Philip lived in their constituency, exercising his gifts in their cities. It is only natural to expect action to match words spoken. The earnest expectation of all creation desires to see an emerging people who will speak the Word of God with the boldness and the same conviction of apostle Paul. He testified to the Corinthians, *"And my speech and my preaching were not with persuasive words of human wisdom, but in demonstration of the Spirit and of power"* (1 Cor. 2:4). Paul was in effect boasting to the measure of the Holy Spirit's presence in his life. He honored the Spirit of God as the reason for the supernatural dimension of power evident in his ministry. Eloquence and fluency of language hindered the Greek's receptiveness of spiritual blessings. As a people of intellectual perception, it would have taken much more than a few conferences to convince those of Corinth of Jesus Christ's saving love, *"For Jews request a sign and Greeks seek after wisdom"* (1 Cor. 1:22).

Apostle Paul ushered believers in Corinth into encounters with the Holy Spirit through his ministry of power; a challenge to believers today. He gave two reasons in First Corinthians 2 that I personally consider to be the bedrock of his achievements in Corinth. I use the word "achievement" in referring to the tangible presence of God manifested through miracles, signs, and wonders. First, Paul was focused on his assignment by determining not to *"know anything among you except Jesus Christ and Him crucified"* (1 Cor. 2:2). Second, he was concerned for the spiritual well-being of his converts: *"that your faith should not be in the wisdom of men but in the power of God"* (1 Cor. 2:5). So in effect, Paul's ambition was to please Jesus, and to train converts who would equally seek to please the Lord rather than men. The is the same challenge of the Issachar Mandate calling for a repositioning of the prophetic gift from the temple to the streets and marketplace.

The Church is recognized in the Bible as *"the pillar and ground of the truth"* (1 Tim. 3:15). To this end, the gathered Church must now earnestly activate the gifts within each member, who as *living stones* will be used to establish the house of God.[98] To achieve this important purpose, the foundation building anointing of apostle and prophet must be fully restored in the Church.[99] The time has now come for the fivefold office functions identified in Ephesians 4 to be fully restored to the Church for greater effectiveness in the mission to make Christ known to the world.

FRESH FIRE FOR A NEW DISPENSATION

As mentioned previously spiritual gifts did not become extinct post early church nor were they limited to that age. As a matter of fact, present spiritual trends reveal new apostolic paradigms positioning the

Church for greater thrusts of God's power. The purpose of the power surge coming to the Church will be to bring all things together in Christ according to Paul's message to the saints in Ephesus.[100] As ambassadors of Christ, our lives should then serve as bridges of hope enabling many despondent in our societies to experience new life. Spiritual inactivity or passivity attracts antibodies that weaken our spiritual immune systems. An inactive body is vulnerable to attacks. Our immunity as children of the living God is in our obedience to His Word. Upon receiving the world commission from Jesus Christ, the early disciples commenced activities to fulfill the promise of divine empowerment. Their obedience won the accreditation of the Holy Spirit: *"And they went out and preached everywhere, the Lord working with them and confirming the word through the accompanying signs"* (Mark 16:20).

The Greek word for "confirming" in Mark 16:20, is *bebaioo* and it means "to make firm, establish, secure, corroborate, guarantee." In other words their obedience secured the establishing power of God throughout their activities. It means their actions were corroborated, secured, made firm, and guaranteed by the Holy Spirit. Similarly, as we obey the command to preach the Gospel to all creatures, our ministries will be accredited by the Holy Spirit's power to effect change in lives and communities. Apostle Paul quite blatantly declared: *"For the kingdom of God is not in word but in power"* (1 Cor. 4:20).

BEARING THE MARK OF CHRIST

Unless issues of responsibility bearing are sorted out, the Church will continue the present trend of dependency or defaulting into idolizing individual ministries. Equally those who have been anointed to serve in lands and nations seduced by idol worshiping may be deceived into believing spiritual gifts are exclusive rights of Christian leadership. A prophet to a nation, nations, or globe is mandated to hear God's heart for their sphere of authority as a matter of service—not choice. It should be demanded of such persons or ministries as a matter of service and not due to carnal ministry recognition. As part of our maturing process, the Church needs to be better equipped to rank prophetic ministries for the sake of effective service to the Body of Christ and responsibility bearing to the world.

I have been privileged to serve as part of prophets' roundtables both at national and continental levels where, through several hours and days, dedicated leaders gather for the sake of the Church and nation (land). Although the gatherings focus primarily on hearing the voice of God with an aim to declare His prophetic word, there is never pressure to hear or speak out. In that regard, the prophets gather as a matter of calling and responsibility but in humility recognizing God's sovereign will to speak—or not to speak. Such roundtables should be encouraged for development of prophetic ministries across prophetic streams for the sake of the corporate mission to make Christ known. Prophetic elderships or councils of accountability need to be established in nations where such bodies are not in function. With prophets in unity, the Church is bound to witness practical releasing of the prophetic gift at all levels of our experience. I also believe the time has come to bridge gaps in the prophetic communities across streams making up the river of God. This is a strong aspect of the Issachar Mandate.

Chapter Five

━┈ ≍◈≍ ┈━

FAITH: UNLOCKING THE SUPERNATURAL REALM

Aim: To reiterate the importance of trusting in the will and
   purpose of God for every believer. Faith is the key that
   unlocks the supernatural realm and releases supernatural abilities in believers as a matter of lifestyle.

*Now faith is the substance of things hoped for, the evidence
of things not seen* (Hebrews 11:1).

Faith activates the gifts and is the key to functioning in the
anointing. If you imagine a stationary car, without a key in the
ignition, the car stays stationary. The function of a car key is to start
its engine, while it takes fuel to run a car. The Holy Spirit is the fuel
powering the human vehicle,[101] but first the faith key must be
inserted into the depths of our hearts to ignite passion for Christ.
Unless a believer receives the revelation of God's sovereignty and
supremacy, such a person will experience difficulties in hoping for the
unusual in their ministry.[102] The supernatural realm is accessed by
faith[103] and operated in a mind-set that works in the opposite of
common sense.[104] On many occasions through the gospels, Jesus

rewarded those who operated in faith.[105] He chastized the disciples for not having faith.[106]

Faith is defined in the Greek by the word *pistis* meaning, "conviction, confidence, trust, belief, reliance, trustworthiness, and persuasion." In the New Testament application, pistis refers to inner confidence, reliance in God, and trust.

I once belonged to a dynamic church congregation in the mid-80s that operated in a dimension of faith Heaven would have acknowledged. The pastor would often shout out from the pulpit: "You have a direct line to God, you have a 999 line; just call and he will answer you." I could engage with the image of a telephone on God's priority table. We were trained to operate in absolute faith. *"But without faith it is impossible to please Him, for he who comes to God must believe that He is"* (Heb. 11:6). I arrived back in London in 1991 after three years abroad with the fire of the Holy Spirit in my belly. With no more than three scriptures in my memory bank I was inspired to pray for an influential lady who had been diagnosed with cancer of the spine. I remember feeling heat waves down my arms as I placed my hand on her back after leading her to the Lord. Thankfully, she was healed and miraculously discharged from hospital three days later. She is still in active ministry.

My faith grew from then, leading me to pray with several cancer cases that received complete healing. On one occasion as I prayed for a woman diagnosed with throat cancer she suddenly rushed to the toilet. I could hear her wretching loudly as though she was vomiting. The Spirit of the Lord revealed she was throwing up the tumor as Brother Hagin, whose ministry greatly impacted my life, would often write about. She later received an all-clear from the hospital. I remember another lady who was a member of the weekly prayer and Bible meetings held at my home. She was healed of sickle cell anemia in 1995 during one of our prayer meetings. She went on to have three sons, with none testing positive for sickle cell, a medical wonder. Her case was subsequently reported in a Canadian medical journal. The same lady was also miraculously healed of a deformity in her left hand sustained in a car crash when she was 17 years old. The healing occurred the same night as the sickle cell and fibroid growths in her womb disappeared, confirming the goodness of our God. Her left hand grew 3 inches—matching her right hand, finger to finger. I will never forget her joy and that of our group.

When asked how it came about, I could only remember a very tall man standing by me, taking hold of my hand and teaching me what to do and where to lay my hand as I prayed for the lady. We need that tall man—Jesus—to minister with us in this dark hour.

OPERATING IN THE SUPERNATURAL REALM

The world has had to endure natural disasters of significant proportions with relief agencies under pressure from a worldwide refugee crisis. With so much hopelessness in the world, the Church must rise up to the challenges at hand to interpret the signs of the times. It is crucial for the children of the living God to fulfill their ambassadorial destiny. Ambassadors[107] represent their nations faithfully and also enjoy immunity from the laws of host nations. As believers in Christ, we must align with heaven for skills to understand the times.[108] The Church is to commence training of the troops to represent efficiently.[109] The power of God in believers needs to manifest through visible signs, miracles, and wonders in active ministry.[110] Such a drive by the Church to fulfill divine purpose would serve to counteract efforts of humanist, Islamic, and other evil agendas seeking to challenge the laws of God. God's heart for all men to come to repentance should be seen as motivation for exercising spiritual gifts in ministry.[111] David questioned the armies of Israel, *"Is there not a cause"* (1 Sam. 17:29).

The Church must push for supernatural power.[112] With all the human wisdom and technological advancements of the Western world, it is yet to be said that prisoners were set loose while praying and singing.[113] The authority of the Kingdom of God testified to through the ministry of the early church ought to be received as spiritual heritage relevant to our present day existence. The Bible recorded the experience of Paul and Silas in prison. While praying and singing hymns to God, *"suddenly there was a great earthquake, so that the foundations of the prison were shaken; and immediately all the doors were opened and everyone's chains were loosed"* (Acts 16:26).

ACTIVE FAITH

No child of God should now be content with living a mundane, ordinary lifestyle.[114] We are God's spiritual power plants, called to change our world with the light of Jesus Christ.[115] As believers in Christ Jesus we inherited new creation status when He shed His blood at Calvary (2 Cor. 5:17). The blood of Jesus won us access[116] to supernatural existence by wiping out the handwriting of accusation that once existed against us.[117] So no matter the circumstances present in the natural experience, access to power with which natural results are reversed has been given to the Church. To activate this authority in Christ, the prophetic church should *"declare a thing, and it will be established for you"* (Job 22:28). It is important to seek understanding of the fullness of blessings we inherited in Christ. Profound supernatural abilities intrinsic to the new life inherited by virtue of the blood of Jesus are readily available to the Body of Christ.[118]

Believers need to go beyond understanding spiritual gifts to manifesting these attributes of God within each of us.[119] The Lord promised His disciples, *"These signs will follow those who believe"* (Mark 16:17). The signs were to be performed "in My name." The name of Jesus invokes supernatural power with which spiritual change is effected.[120]

ALL THINGS ARE POSSIBLE

But Jesus looked at them and said, *"with men it is impossible, but not with God; for with God all things are possible"* (Mark 10:27).

Faith necessary to operate spiritual gifts is determined by an individual's ability to trust God implicitly.[121] Faith is operated by a firm persuasion borne out of conviction.[122] Conviction necessary to operate faith is inspired by knowledge of God's infallible word: *"Faith comes by hearing and hearing by the word of God"* (Rom. 10:17). Compassion is another ingredient necessary to operate a ministry of power. Jesus was often moved by compassion as was recorded in Scripture.[123] His followers should resolve to engage with the works of Christ. Apostle Paul pronounced, *"For the love of Christ compels us"* (2 Cor. 5:14). The prophetic gift in active use will certainly enhance the Church's efforts to defeat *"the rulers of the darkness of this age"* (Eph. 6:12).

I was asked an interesting question during a recent supernatural dialogue with the Spirit of the Lord. I was asked: "What *quality* would you say characterized My ministry?" Excitedly, I answered "love." After all Jesus epitomized love, I thought to myself; so my answer made sense. He whispered into my heart "compassion." I was not entirely wrong but it was compassion Jesus was waiting to hear. As followers of Jesus Christ we are told to have compassion for the needs of others in society.[124] It was compassion that led Jesus to heal the sick and cast out devils.[125] Compassion for the unsaved, the homeless, and the deprived in our communities should inspire believers to become a praying, fasting, worshiping Church.[126] God's supernatural empowerment works to the benefit of others.[127] Jesus Christ's mission on earth was for the benefit of humanity.[128] Now His Church is being called by the Spirit of God to offer our lives corporately as tunnels of love for the sake of others who must access the gift of salvation.

WE MUST DECREASE

The Issachar Mandate is a revolutionary call to the Church to interpret her times in tune with changing times and epoch. John the Baptist's assignment was to prepare a people for the coming of the Lord in fulfillment of Isaiah's prophecy.[129] John did not at any time draw attention to his ministry, instead he focused the Jews on the One who was to come.[130] There is a generation of righteous leadership being called forth.[131] They will not fear to loose their heads at the appropriate time for a people to come through into God's redemptive purpose. The Church can no longer operate on man-engineered agendas. The Issachar Mandate demands we read the times and align with God's prophetic clock. Unfortunately, a large section of the Church is distracted by personal agendas. However, God will not bless works of flesh that bear no resemblance to his heart.[132] Faith, an attribute of God's manifold wisdom, remains an enemy of human wisdom.[133] To push through to the realm of power where the Church sees prophecy and other spiritual gifts manifesting through every believer will require faith.[134]

Overcoming the Greek Mind-set

Apostle Paul still managed to plant churches in Corinth, a place where human wisdom, or the Greek mind-set, prevailed. He challenged:

> *Where is the wise? Where is the scribe? Where is the disputer of this age? Has God not made foolish the wisdom of this world? For since in the wisdom of God, the world through wisdom did not know God, it pleased God through the foolishness of the message preached to save those who believe* (1 Corinthians 1:20-21).

As simple as the statement, *"For since in the wisdom of God, the world through wisdom did not know God"* sounds, the truth revealed is quite deep and not necessarily for this book. Paul is also speaking to those who in our time still prefer to allow the Greek mind-set to stand in the way of the life ordained for believers. God was not about to arm wrestle with the Greeks who were wise in their own eyes, and He will not do so with believers in our time. Because God is the "I AM," He was not suddenly going to be an analytical, human reasoning God, just to match up with the Greek mind-set. He frustrated human wisdom through the foolishness of the Cross.[135]

The new interpretative role demanded of the Church calls particularly for strategies to overcome antichrist agendas. In order to frustrate "Greek reasoning" challenge in any spiritual climate with obvious signs of worship of the intellect, the Church must operate in the humility of the Cross. The folly of human wisdom is exposed in the foolishness of the Cross. *"For the message of the cross is foolishness to those who are perishing, but to us who are being saved it is the power of God"* (1 Cor. 1:18).

Chapter Six

INTIMACY WITH CHRIST

Aim: To emphasize the importance of maintaining a lifestyle of intimacy with Christ.

FULFILLING PROPHETIC DESTINY

And the Spirit and the bride say, "Come!" And let him who hears say, "Come!" And let him who thirsts come. Whoever desires, let him take the water of life freely (Revelation 22:17).

Prophecy reveals the heart of God.[136] To prophesy the heart of God one must be connected to God in an experience of continual love and affection.[137] Passion for Christ drives any prophetic ministry in the right direction, all the time pointing His people to the love of Jesus.[138] The prophetic heart is a heart of worship[139] among other dynamics. Prophecy goes beyond foretelling and forth telling into dimensions we are yet to discover as the Lord's prophetic clock unfolds.[140] We need to activate more radical, extreme prophetic such as existed in Elisha's ministry. The enemies of divine purpose need to confess: "*Elisha, the prophet who is in Israel, tells the King of Israel the words that you speak in your bedroom"* (2 Kings 6:12). Radical youth culture who speak the language of Jeremiah, *"But His word was in my heart like a burning fire, shut up in my bones,"*[141] need to be equipped for the work of the ministry.

The Church as the Bride of Christ needs to be the expression of Christ's prophetic ministry on the earth. We should serve as guiding lights in communities and to governments.

A GREAT CLOUD OF WITNESSES

Therefore we also, since we are surrounded by so great a cloud of witnesses, let us lay aside every weight, and the sin which so easily ensnares us, and let us run with endurance the race that is set before us (Hebrews 12:1).

I was impacted by details of an open vision I had several years ago.[142] As I looked I realized I was watching a room full of wedding guests. They anxiously waited for the marriage ceremony to commence. The ceremony was taking place in a beautiful ballroom. I became more interested as I recognized two of the guests—Kathryn Kuhlman and Smith Wigglesworth. As I continued watching I realized the wedding guests were faithful servants of old. The groom stood alone on the front row. Now and again, the guests would look toward the double doors at the back of the ballroom in anticipation. My own anticipation grew as I watched. Suddenly, the double doors opened, and although there were no sounds yet I could hear the joy of their hearts. The bride was escorted by someone but I could not make out who this person was because He is the Holy Spirit. I could not believe what I saw next. Although the bridegroom did not look back when the double doors flung open, He seemed to know exactly[143] when His bride would stand besides Him.

Suddenly the bridegroom and His bride linked arms in the most amazing picture of love. Immediately, the great cloud of witnesses jumped to their feet, every one, and joined in the most beautiful dance—the dance of the Groom and his Bride. There was no formal marriage ceremony, although the Bride was dressed in a white gown.

"He who has the bride is the bridegroom"(John 3:29). The Church, the Bride of Christ is being prepared for her Bridegroom. We are not alone but are surrounded by the witness of those who toiled for such a time as this. It is for their sakes we must now embrace the mandate of our mission.[144]

Creation cries out: *"For we know that the whole creation groans and labors with birth pangs together until now"* (Rom. 8:22).

With so much disenfranchisement and disillusionment in the world, there is a cry from the earth for justice. The heavenly hosts appear to be calling out for greater partnership from the Church.[145] We are being called to arms, to dislodge the forces of darkness threatening the advancement of the Kingdom of God[146] as a matter of responsibility.[147]

Ezekiel, a prophet, was placed in a valley full of dry bones by the Spirit of God and asked to prophesy. The bones were described as *"very dry,"* yet the Lord spoke to Ezekiel, *"Prophesy to these bones, and say to them, 'O dry bones, hear the word of the Lord'"* (Ezek. 37:2,4). God has not given up on the unsaved among the saved, hence He seeks labourers in his vineyard.[148] The prophetic gift needs to be deployed in every direction in obedience to the corporate commission of the Church. Jesus Christ, a prophet said, *"I must work the works of Him who sent Me while it is day; the night is coming when no one can work"* (John 9:4). His followers ought to imbibe the essence of His words with time-conscious measures that keep followers focused on our primary calling.

It is a fact that nations and governments founded on Christian heritage are being held ransom by false religions, philosophies, and ideologies that contravene the Word of God.[149]

Gay lobbyists are intensifying campaigns for equal civil rights and social benefits for same sex marriages as God's ordained order for holy matrimony. Political correctness, not prophecy, appears to be shaping our world. The Bible warns there is *"one Lawgiver, who is able to save and to destroy"* (James 4:12).

Interpreting the Wars of Our Time

The Church as a prophetic community needs to corporately engage more purposefully with issues of morality. Clear biblical counsel[150] should be offered at all times, unlike the mixed sounds that leave the Body of Christ looking like a divided army.[151] Increasingly, many will look to the prophetic community for interpretation whenever disasters occur. Is the Church poised to assist the world in this evil day?

I sensed the role of the prophetic mantle was changing to more of an interpretative emphasis when the Lord spoke to me concerning England during July 2005. The message was to "prayerfully watch for every seventh day in July." The instructions given did not indicate mine and others prayers would avert impending danger. However, prayers of the saints contained the evil plans of the enemy as the unfolding of the events confirmed. Later on in the month I discerned the Spirit of the Lord was calling on the Church to look to Him for interpretation of the events unfolding before us.[152]

On July 7, 2005, there was a terrorist bomb attack on London, a foiled attempt on the 21st and a freak tornado in Birmingham on the 28th. Only one seventh day in July—July 14—was without a disaster, or near disaster. The Lord desires to whisper His secrets into our ears.[153]

My attention was drawn particularly to the unexpected tornado in Birmingham on July 28, 2005. I felt a sense of responsibility toward the Church as one called to serve in the prophetic ministry. I knew to seek the Lord for insight into an incident I discerned to be a manipulation of weather by evil forces. The Lord confirmed my fears as my eyes were opened to a type of civil war among members of the community affected. Grievances relating to the aborted terrorist attack against London were being sorted out by humans who knew how to fight using weather elements. The natural manifestations and spiritual effects of this invincible warfare could be easily interpreted by the grace of God. House roofs in the affected areas appeared to have been specifically targeted. A clear message was sent to a people who I suspect understood it. Such spiritual battles engaging the firmament are common in West Africa, where lightning, thunder, and storms are employed by occultists and used against unsuspecting targets.

Elijah, the man of faith and prayer confronted weather elements when he declared, *"There shall not be dew nor rain these years except at my word"* (1 Kings 17:1). I believe the Body of Christ in the Western world will increasingly be required to confront high-ranking demonic principalities that will intend to *"change times, and law"* (Dan. 7:25). These are the evil forces that now contend weather-related prophecies and prophetic utterances in some parts of Europe.

One obvious consequence of immigration, trade pacts, and other means of international cooperation is the people mix in our present day societies. A new global community is forming around the earth with spiritual and natural implications such as previously identified that cannot be ignored by the prophetic community. Fortunately, all authority has been given to the Church with which to serve the Lord. Followers of Christ possess tremendous spiritual leverage in the blood of Jesus.

INTERPRETING TRAUMA

Effective prayer strategies can only be formulated by an army able to identify an enemy or enemies. Believers, being true worshipers of the Lord, are to focus primarily on our call to worship. Revelation flows out of the place of intimacy and worship of our Lord. The Lord spoke to me recently about the coming global revival through the Body of Christ. He said this revival will begin at a personal level and be multiplied through the lives of individuals, who will carry the light of Christ. Trauma was revealed as a major stronghold that will be broken in the seasons ahead. With this will come deliverance of many children and young adults from autism and other communication disorders rooted in trauma suffered in and out of the womb. The Lord also spoke of trauma to nations (lands) and the implication of bloodshed on a land. Trauma causes dislocation or separation, spiritual and natural, leaving room for initiation of satanic rule through subsequent lawlessness. Apostolic decrees and declarations should be made with the intention to cancel out the effects of trauma as mentioned on a land. Prophets are required to assist the Church by interpreting the trends and signs of our ever-evolving societies.

To combat and negate the plans of the demonic to harvest seeds of trauma and bloodshed, Christian leaders and intercessors should stand at the exact points to overrule demonic decrees. If gaps created through trauma are not closed, such spots as points of initial trauma are likely to be used as "contact points" for the enemy's ploys. Evil covenants allowed to root by the Church's ignorance will invite a reign of lawlessness—a clear agenda of the antichrist.

The Church needs to prepare an apostolic and prophetic praying army who must intensify prayer for the lost in our communities.[154]

INTERPRETING WAR SEASONS

I strongly believe that the shock experienced in 2005 by the British land (London bombings) on July 7 (7/7) became a point of contact for initiating a 7-year season of war. The spiritual wars of our time have been allowed for a purpose—not for the devil's glory but for the birthing of a glorious Church. Daniel's visions of the beasts described a time when the horn representing a fourth world power was making war against the saints. The horn prevailed until *"the Ancient of Days came...the time came for the saints to possess the kingdom"* (Dan. 7:22). For a time in Persia it seemed Haman had succeeded in his evil plot against the Jews until Esther was made to recognize she may have been in the Kingdom *"for such a time as this"* (Esther 4:14).

Revelation chapter 12 opens with, *"Now a great sign appeared in heaven."* After that sign is interpreted in the next verse another sign is revealed: *"And another sign appeared in heaven"* (verse 3). This sign was of a great, fiery, red dragon having seven heads and ten horns, and seven diadems on his heads. The dragon appeared to challenge divine purpose by attempting to devour the Child of a woman who was ready to give birth. The Church then flees into the wilderness, "where she has a place prepared by God" (Rev. 12:6).

The woman, representing the Church of Christ, was protected by God as the angelic hosts engaged the dragon and his angels. It appears the Church is now being prepared for the earthly version of the war we read about in the Heavens. The invincible war had prepared an overcoming army that would overcome the great dragon "by the blood of the Lamb and the word of their testimony", not loving their lives to the death (Rev. 12:11). It is important for the prophetic church from nation to nation to interpret their war seasons, else casualties will emerge from out-of-time wars. We now need to partner more strategically with the angelic hosts for the wars of our time. Daniel was given skills of interpretation of the apocalyptic visions; he was given understanding (Dan. 8:16).

Strategic level spiritual warfare networks need to be established globally with the sole purpose of destroying demonic plans aimed at unleashing lawlessness on the earth. The devil is persistent and continues to further his objectives through violence. If not challenged, the demonic calendar for England in particular and other nations of Britain is set at fulfilling an agenda by the end of 2012.

The global Church has been armed with the requisite spiritual authority in God's Word to intercept and destroy the plans of the evil one.[155] Our war is against an enemy whose various identities were uncovered in the Word of God.[156] The Church needs to discern and understand what the enemy of our souls wants at this present time in order to determine his failure.[157] Daniel had to press into God in a dark hour[158] such as our world is faced with for his nation's deliverance.

The season of spiritual war began in the United States with 9/11 according to interpretation offered widely by Chuck Pierce, a respected global prophet. The war season was reported as a 7-year war. This period can now be interpreted as ending in 2008. The church in the United States should now employ and deploy the prophetic gift in an attempt to decipher the enemy's plans. Going by the pattern I have understood with which the demonic calendar of the antichrist is unfolding, the prophetic church in the U.S.A. must interpret the end of this season of war, so that the devil is denied access to his next plan (Prov. 26:2). War seasons are times when the enemy is allowed to use his best weapons so that the army of God familiarize themselves with his armory. However, the devil should not be allowed to drag out spiritual wars, nor determine when they end.

The Lord will strengthen the praying army to turn away spiritual battles at their nation's gate.[159] Strategic prayer warriors in the U.S.A. should assume a corporate posture of intense prayer to destroy any convergence of demonic powers targeting a harvest of evil in 2008. Elijah *"bowed down on the ground, and put his face between his knees"* to see his prophetic word come to pass.[160] The same posture can prevent the enemy from gaining entrance into lives and nations. The prophetic gift arms believers to receive deep secrets from God's heart for the day of evil.[161]

The Lord also spoke to me concerning patterns and cycles of the enemy's systems of operation. From nation to nation, the Church is to watch and pray for destruction of the enemy's plans. Other nations observed include Nigeria, a nation standing on the same spiritual timeline as Britain, which suffered trauma to her land through a plane crash on October 22, 2005 (10/22). That day began Nigeria's 7-year season of war in confirmation of a prophetic word I gave some in government in that nation. Since then, lawlessness has increased with previously unimaginable acts of violence including a car bomb attack. Also in 2005, France experienced senseless fires that engulfed apartment blocks in Paris to the shock of the world. Once again, issues relating to immigration and immigrants were identified at the heart of France's trauma. The world is in a time for the Issachar Mandate, a time for prophetic engagement.

A NEW DAWNING

The prophetic church needs to call for a season upon the Church and nations similar to the days of Joseph[162] and Daniel, when men in authority will have dreams that can only be interpreted by people in covenant with God.[163] We need divine strategies to stand strong in a time of terrible darkness covering the earth. I have noticed a trend suggesting this season of dreams is upon the Church of Christ. On three occasions so far, I have received knowledge of the plans of the enemy including uncovering of one case of entrenched ancestral witchcraft through dreams. The Lord is allowing the pride in the hearts of men to be exposed through their ambitious dreams while also revealing deep secrets to His faithful ones through dreams.

All Creation Is Waiting

For the earnest expectation of the creation eagerly waits for the revealing of the sons of God (Romans 8:19).

With so much uncertainty in the world around us, it is hardly surprising that many people are desperate to make sense of upheavals, uprisings, and general crisis. Questions being asked through news media may be interpreted as: *"Where is God,"* or *"Where was God when this happened?"* The voice of the antichrist can be heard through the questions asked on secular platforms. The main objective of the enemy is to deceive believers in Christ and the unsaved to question God's deity.[164]

The earnest expectation of society, the unsaved, is for the prophetic church to come to terms with their ordained authority to deliver whole cities from bondage.[165] The gift of prophecy has been given by the Holy Spirit to *"a holy nation,"*[166] to be used strategically for sake of salvation. It is important for the Church in this new dawning to re-examine past activities in order to assume present responsibility. The Church has at times operated on a "here is what our God says; take it or leave it" type mandate. But there is now a new paradigm, a fresh call for clarity of communication if we are to impact our communities. As the call of the Issachar Mandate or prophetic engagement is focused on the equipping of the saints for the work of ministry, it is important for the equippers to avoid the errors of the past.

Christians very often practice what I term "selective hearing," only receiving partial aspects of a message that suited their circumstance. Sometimes people twisted words to their advantage all the time seeking comfort zones that neither challenged attitude or lifestyle. I remember the days of "name it, claim it" declarations. Believers were encouraged to "give to receive," a biblical fact. Some in the Body of Christ sought to thwart the Scriptures to suit unrighteous expectations. The rebellious among us believed God could be manipulated to grant spiritual harvests regardless of lifestyle.

My four times trained legal mind could not cope with the faith expectancy of such believers who conveniently twist words of preachers. I needed someone to help me interpret some of the messages I heard preached. I knew faith was the substance of things hoped for, evidence of things not seen, but I recognized that faith allowed for practicality. The fact that an offering is dropped in a basket did not serve as license to sin and expect a harvest. I was bothered by my opinion—not knowing whether I was right or wrong to entertain such thoughts, I resorted to amusing myself. I would chuckle naughtily in the safety of my bedroom, imagining myself a mortgage lender, and at the end of the month responding to a *"name it, claim it"* Christian borrower. My response would have been, *"you took it, you pay it!"* God is faithful but not to be mocked.[167] Any person desiring to practice their gift of prophecy should assess their lives in the light of the experience of the seven sons of Sceva.[168] The Church is the earthly expression of God. Our task is to make sure Joe and Jane Anybody understands this nature is, in effect, God on the earth.

WE ARE CONNECTED

The Lord is not disconnected from His Bride, nor should the Bride be disconnected from her Bridegroom. The hour has come to link arms with the Bridegroom: *"And the Spirit and the bride say 'Come!' And let him who hears say 'Come!'"* (Rev. 22:17).

The onus is on the Bride of Christ to show love, teach love, and live love—an important foundation to effective prophetic ministry. Apostle Paul taught, *"Pursue love, and desire spiritual gifts, but especially that you may prophecy"* (1 Cor. 14:1). It is believers who are to transmit light wherever darkness prevails.[169] As a matter of fact, Jesus through His teachings implored his disciples to be *"light."* He taught, *"You are the light of the world"* (Matt. 5:14).

A house may be connected to electricity, yet the people live in darkness. A household will be in darkness if the light bulbs and light switches are not in functioning order. The prophetic Bride of Christ, the Church, is called to be light in our communities. However, unless Christ, the light of the world, is transmitted from His Church to the world, our cities will remain covered by darkness.

Jesus is love; He epitomized love. He lived out love through His ministry of compassion, healing the sick and casting out devils from those oppressed. Jesus was connected to His Father and to the Holy Spirit (John 10:30). He announced the source of His supernatural ministry at the start of His ministry (Luke 4:18).

POWER IS COMING TO THE CHURCH

I had cause to share details of a visitation I had in 2001, when the Lord appeared to announce the coming of His power to the Church.[170] I told the details to Dr. Sharon Predovitch, a dynamic apostle and mentor, who after listening intently, handed me a book written by the late Dr. Fuschia Pickett. The book detailed an account of a vision she had years before of a power plant—speaking of revival coming to the Church. Fuschia Pickett's documented vision mirrored-imaged the international business the Lord blessed me with when I was called to full-time ministry. I remember an important instruction from the visitation quite distinctly: "You have to learn to generate, distribute, and transmit this energy." I am now in my sixth year of marketing materials used for energy generation, distribution, and transmission to a national grid.

With the benefit of business engagement I can confirm a need to prepare for an upsurge of God's power. The Lord wants the Church to acquire strategic knowledge for future advancement of the Kingdom. Through the functions of electricity equipment I deal with such as surge arrestors, lightening arrestors, clamps, termination kits, and the like so I can appreciate the coming power to God's house. In effect my business is a manifestation of Dr. Pickett's vision, a prophetic experience of a woman years beforehand in the U.S.A.

Power is coming to the Body of Christ but, as the Lord said, we have to learn to generate, distribute, and transmit energy to homes as electricity that gives comfort. A dimension of the prophetic gift is to serve as light bulbs shining the glory of the Lord in outward manifestation. Prophecy serves as God's transmission line offering comfort, encouragement, and hope for the future.[171] The Bride of Christ is being called by the Spirit to approach Heaven with unveiled faces. As we press into God in transparency, beholding as in a mirror the glory of the Lord, we too will be transformed by the fire of His holiness, made ready for the Master's use.[172] The Bride must now call out to the Spirit in partnership for the sake of those who perish through sin and rebellion to God. Together the voice of God must be heard through our acts of kindness, inspired by his Spirit saying *"Come."*[173]

SEEK HIM FIRST

But seek first the kingdom of God and His righteousness, and all these things shall be added to you (Matthew 6:33).

So far the focus of the prophetic church has been centered on internal matters of housekeeping. Pastors of local churches are weighed down with immature Christians who make counseling sessions busy. The hour has come to equip the saints to know Jesus as the Counselor,[174] Healer,[175] Warrior,[176] and Savior.[177] The saints need to be prepared, to be equipped to serve as human channels for transmission of divine power.[178] The time has come now more than ever to transform the lives of those we have been commissioned to reach. But first the prophetic church needs to be refined by the fire of His holiness.[179] The entire army of Christ needs to be mobilized to function in a real world as light and as salt.[180]

A PICTURE OF HIS LOVE

...not willing that any should perish but that all should come to repentance... (2 Peter 3:9).

88

When the Lord stood over my bed in His glory to call me into His service, I could only do one thing, hide from the awesome brilliance of the light in my room. I tried hiding under my double divan bed from the humbling power of His radiance. I will never forget the dialogue that followed, a picture of His love and mercy. Jesus reminded me of a book I read in 1988 and my innermost thoughts at the time. The book was about a Muslim woman born to a prominent family in Islamabad, Pakistan. She was born crippled and despite many trips to several Islamic holy places, like Mecca and Medina, she did not receive the hoped-for healing. Then she was given a Bible by an evangelist, which she began to read. The story went on to reveal a visitation from the Lord. Jesus taught her to recite the words of the Lord's Prayer[181] and when she had done as she was told, He simply asked her to "rise up and walk." Her healing caused so much uproar and embarrassment for her influential Muslim family that they tried to persuade her to renounce Jesus as her healer. Eventually she was disowned by her family after declining their request. She chose Jesus Christ over her natural inheritance.

My passion for Jesus was stirred by this amazing picture of His love, and victory over false gods. I believe the Church can activate the resident anointing in the testimony of this lady who became an evangelist. I did so by praying in 1998 for the same experience as the Muslim lady. The quiet prayers of my heart were answered five years later in 1993 when the Lord appeared in glory in my room. I could hardly stand or sit in the brilliance of the light in my room. He reminded me of the innermost thoughts of my heart. The thoughts of our hearts are known to God, so also should the thoughts of His heart be revealed in and through His Church. Jesus recorded the thoughts I had, thoughts known to no one else. The Lord recorded thoughts I had in 1988 only to recite them back to me on April 17, 1993.

The Church, Christ's prophetic Bride, is being called into new levels of intimacy with the Bridegroom. The gifts of the Spirit are operated out of intimacy. The Church cannot afford to function outside of wedlock but to receive empowerment by the touch of His kiss. Jesus touched the Muslim lady with His love and she walked. He reached out to her she held His hands and walked. He simply taught her to call out *"Your kingdom come, Your will be done on earth as it is in heaven"* (Luke 11:2-3).

The love of Christ also unlocks the gate to supernatural experiences.[182] What we cannot afford as a Body is an experience without the Master. There is a call for true worshipers, those who will worship Christ in spirit and truth[183] not for spiritual gifts. Our motivation for seeking prophetic power needs to be in check at all times. The prophetic Bride of Christ is a servant church, placing the needs of others above her own. Jesus had no place to sleep, begged for water,[184] and retreated into lonely places for prayer.[185] We must become more mission minded to fulfill the corporate mandate of the Church.[186]

> *"For the testimony of Jesus is the spirit of prophecy"* (Revelation 19:10).

Chapter Seven

⚜

PARTNERING WITH HEAVEN

Aim: To emphasize the importance of maintaining an intimate
relationship with the Lord Jesus—as His earthly representatives. Our focus should be on the Giver of spiritual
gifts and not on the gifts.

Every prophetic ministry or ministry seeking to operate in the supernatural dimension of power must cultivate intimate relationship
with the Lord Jesus Christ. Our ministries must be modeled after the
Lord's. A well-trained prophetic army will need to function in the Issachar anointing to understand the times and the strategies of God to
advance His Kingdom in their communities.[187] Jesus was baptized as
"the Holy Spirit descended in bodily form like a dove upon Him"
(Luke 3:22). He was anointed for ministry by the Holy Spirit as He
testified, *"The Spirit of the Lord is upon Me, because He has anointed
Me"* (Luke 4:18). Jesus was also *"led by the Spirit into the wilderness"* (Luke 4:1) to be tempted in preparation for ministry and when
the time was up, *"Jesus returned in the power of the Spirit to Galilee"*
(Luke 4:14).

The key to effective ministry is in maintaining contact with Heaven.[188] Jesus only did what He saw His Father do (John 5:19). Fleshly exploits of carnal inducement do not carry spiritual authority in the heavens; perpetrators are soon attacked by the host of evil.[189] Our spiritual wars are not against humans but against principalities and powers in heavenly places.[190] Spiritual wars are not to be fought with earthly weapons.[191] Several men in the Bible engaged Heaven in intercession for divine intervention in times of difficulty.

The prophetic gift ensured supernatural breakthrough for men such as Daniel[192], Apostle Paul[193], and others of the early church. The Church as a prophetic community needs to function corporately in tenacity of mind necessary to unseat satanic domains in our nations.[194] Jesus disarmed satan and his evil coalition by confronting him in his own territory.[195] The enemy of the Church, satan, is still at work in our societies. The enemy of men's souls maintains continual grip on lives of *"the sons of disobedience"* through drugs, sin, and general rebellion to the ways of God (see Eph. 2:2). It is for the sake of these ones the Church must reassess existing strategies for evangelism. John was invited to a higher place to receive revelation shortly after the message of the Lord to the angels of the seven churches in the Book of Revelation. The Church needs to respond to that voice *"like a trumpet,"* receiving the opportunity to, *"Come up here, and I will show you things which must take place after this"* (Rev. 4:1). The teaching gift in the Church is invaluable but now the rest of the five-fold gifts need to be restored fully to the Church. The Body of Christ has tended to worship knowledge rather than seek revelation, but the Bible warns: *"Knowledge puffs up"* (1 Cor. 8:1); *"for the letter kills, but the Spirit gives life"* (2 Cor. 3:6).

FORGET STRUCTURE, FULFILL DESTINY

As long as the mind-set of the Church is set on maintaining programs and structures, supernatural exploits designed for outside ministry will elude us. Although prophecy at a foundational level is for corporate and personal edification there is room for outdoor application as the case of the early church exemplifies. Early-church apostles such as Paul and

Silas, and disciples such as Philip, applied prophecy to shift paradigms. My challenge to the Church revolves around one thought, *"Pushing boundaries in order to establish the Kingdom of God in our daily experience."* Since every believer possesses the innate ability to exercise prophecy as with other gifts of the Holy Spirit, the need now is for equipping in correct function in spiritual gifts.

We need to move toward more generalized dynamic street outreaches that change environments. Prayer warriors need to walk the streets once more to redeem the land.[196] I believe there are times to stay in prayer closets; but there are also times of manifestation.[197] Manifestation is when power generated in the prayer closet is distributed to the right channels. The world is waiting to experience greater manifestation of God's power through His children.[198] Radical prophetic voices in spheres of government and commerce should be encouraged and armed to combat pressure from spiritists, psychics, and other new age ideologies. Nature abhors vacuums—so does the spiritual realm. The devil thrives in vacuums. The time to speak into hopelessness and to bring change in people is now more than ever.

Building to Pattern

No man or woman of God can establish an enduring work for God unless such is built according to divine pattern. Moses was given exact dimensions for the Tabernacle (Exod. 26).

Noah was also given exact dimensions for the ark he was to construct (Gen. 6:14-16). Prophetic ministries must be modeled after Jesus' prophetic ministry. Jesus testified publicly of His partnership with His Father. He only did what He saw His Father do (John 5:19). He informed the Pharisees who accused Him of bearing witness for Himself, *"For I am not alone, but I am with the Father who sent me"* (John 8:16). Jesus spoke as He heard of His Father, and He did nothing of Himself. Jesus testified, *"But as My Father taught Me, I speak these things"* (John 8:28). His partnership with the Holy Spirit was apparent as narrated at the beginning of this chapter. Jack Deere[199] referred to this profound relationship of humility and unity in his writing on the prophetic ministry.

In Jack's words, "Jesus Himself and His apostles all attribute the divine power in His ministry not to the uniqueness of His deity, but rather to the ministry of the Holy Spirit through Him."

His disciples followed this principle of obedience. Jesus counseled them to, *"Tarry in the city of Jerusalem until you are endued with power from on high"* (Luke 24:49). He did not leave His disciples wondering about the source of the power to drive the vision He was bequeathing. In the instructing words to the disciples Jesus revealed the depth of the partnership of the Trinity. The Holy Spirit to come was *"the Promise of My Father."* Jesus was truly submitted to that divine partnership.[200] The Holy Spirit would empower the apostles for wider ministry.[201] When the appointed time had come, the apostles received divine power from on high, just as the Lord said. The Bible recorded: *"There appeared to them divided tongues, as of fire, and one sat upon each of them"* (Acts 2:3). Acts chapter 2 gives enough detail to appreciate the fact of individuality in the corporate empowerment of the group. There was corporate gifting: *"There appeared to them divided tongues,"* and also individual empowerment, *"and one sat upon each of them."* This must be read as a confirmation of the relevance of each member of the Body of Christ. Each believer carries the glory of God inside of their lives.

WHO ARE YOU?

Every believer in Christ who has a relationship with the Lord ought to expect to be used for divine purpose.[202] The harvest truly is plentiful now more than ever, and the army of God is being called to assume a position of warfare to dispossess the enemy of his claims on the lives of God's creatures. Every member of God's household of faith qualifies to manifest spiritual gifts and to operate in supernatural power for the sake of the lost. Many disqualify themselves for all sorts of reasons, while some have become disqualified through sin, until repentance—*"For the temple of God is holy, which temple you are"*(1 Cor. 3:17). No matter how ill equipped a child of God feels, they deserve to be used in the Kingdom for the sake of souls hanging in the balance. The Holy Spirit, the giver also of spiritual gifts, lives inside of us: *"Or do you not know that your body is the temple of the Holy Spirit who is in you, whom you have from God, and you are not your own"* (1 Cor. 6:19).

With so much scriptural and practical reasons given for divine partnership, there appears to be no apparent reason for the Church not to manifest extraordinary abilities in the course of mission. I am currently working on a personal challenge to seek the Lord for divine empowerment to speak prophetically through daily devotionals for 365 days. If psychics are able to predict events through annual calendars, with reasonable accuracy, I fail to see why the Church relegates divine authority. So long as motives are honorable before God, the Spirit of God desires to vindicate the Church through unusual manifestations of power as was in the case of apostle Paul whose handkerchiefs healed by proxy.[203]

Who Is He?

The writer of the Book of Hebrews reminds believers in Christ Jesus of the secret to functioning in the supernatural—to *"believe that He is."* To pursue the call of God without His presence is the greatest mistake any believer can make. Our obedience activates the prophetic anointing. When Saul fell short of God's direction, he was afflicted by a distressing spirit.[204] Saul symbolizes the flesh, the carnal nature. Any believer who chooses to operate their gift of prophecy outside of Christ runs a risk of bringing themselves under a curse.[205] A perverted prophetic ministry transfers perversion and spiritual death (Rom. 8:6). Moses recognized the significance of being accompanied by the tangible presence of God on the difficult task as that for which he was called.[206] How could Moses lead a rebellious people or minister with distinction without Yahweh's manifest presence? It is time for the prophetic church to mortify the flesh and banish carnality from her activities in this day of the Lord. A corporate call for return of the ark of the Lord needs to be heard from the house of God. We need the presence of God with us as the Church advances into the streets and marketplace with extreme prophecy and prophetic manifestations. This is the charge of the Issachar Mandate.

I live in a region fast becoming a favorite for homosexuals, sex trade, and drug gangs. Our city enjoys a blend of cultures from the cosmopolitan dwellers, an example of modern-day living. With the culture mix of the 21st century come new challenges for the Body of Christ to discern strategies for reaching the lost. I believe one important role the Church in the Western world will be required to play is that of "negotiators." We are confronted with issues of confusion of cultures and beliefs that need to be interpreted for harmonious co-existence. It is alleged that the heir to the English monarch Prince Charles expressed an interest to be known as a "Defender of Faiths" regardless of the Christian heritage of Britain. Moses humbly asked of God, *"If Your presence does not go with us, do not bring us up from here. For how then will it be known that Your people and I have found grace in Your sight, except You go with us?"* (Exod. 33:15-16).

As we serve the purposes of God in our communities the presence of God will be released to pierce the terrible darkness many live under. The Church must now open portals of blessing for cities, towns, and nations.

Chapter Eight

SPIRITUAL GIFTS

Aim: To highlight the diversity of spiritual gifts given to the Church by the Father, Christ, and the Holy Spirit. To encourage and activate born-again believers in their divine right to exercise spiritual gifts as a matter of course in practical ministry.

ALL ONBOARD!

The time has come for the Body of Christ to function in greater dimension of God's power, to release men and women in our communities held captive by forces of evil (Matt. 28:19). All creation is waiting for the display of supernatural power from the house of God through His children (Rom. 8:19). The earth seems to be groaning with birth pangs as recent world disasters reveal. People seek answers to questions in a bid to interpret shifts in the heavens as with the tsunami disaster in Asia. The Body of Christ as a prophetic community must be spiritually positioned to be a sign of God's supremacy on the earth. The Church must revisit priorities in the light of commission in order to answer the present call for the equipping of the saints for the work of ministry. Unless the Body of Christ becomes more mission minded, and less power seeking, the essence of our calling is lost. We need to be light on the earth and a threat to the devil's coalition of evil contending for the hearts of the unsaved.

The Church has been entrusted with a corporate mandate to serve our communities: *"Preach the gospel to creature"* (Mark 16:15). Embedded in our corporate mandate are individual responsibilities to serve more specific objectives such as praying for a nation. It is paramount that the heart of all we do in the name of the Lord serves one common purpose: "to make Jesus Christ known." The Kingdom of God is to be expressed through the Body of Christ. In times past when Jesus taught, preached, and healed, the need to reach out to a wider constituency of Jews was apparent in His statement concerning the harvest. He said, *"The harvest truly is great, but the laborers are few; therefore pray the Lord of the harvest to send out laborers into His harvest"* (Luke 10:2).

Jesus released 70 people into ministry at one point sending them into *"every city and place"* where He was about to go (Luke 10:1). Souls of many around us hang in the balance as spiritual darkness covers the earth through unrighteous, rebellious, and lawless nature exhibited in humans at present. The antichrist's agenda appears to be gaining ground as one nation after another promulgates laws in direct opposition to the laws of our God. The Lord is longsuffering toward His children, *"not willing that any should perish but that all should come to repentance"* (2 Pet. 3:9). Destiny must be fulfilled and so God is patient with us to see His Church rise up in power as the prophetic community we are mandated to be.

The time has come to equip the saints, time for the Church to take stock and to sort out our spiritual houses. But first, the equippers are to be identified in order for the saints to receive genuine training for mission. I am aware of some in the hierarchy of the Church who believe spiritual gifts were done away with the apostles. If that were the case then the portions of the Bible that give impetus for present truth should be obliterated. Apostle Paul distinguished the Church in

Ephesus as being built on *"the foundation of the apostles and prophets, Jesus Christ Himself being the chief cornerstone"* (Eph. 2:20). If true biblical pattern were to be followed, the present church age ought to expect greater apostolic power than the New Testament experience. But then the need to prepare those who must manifest this power in real life experience is greater now than ever.

THE GIFTS OF THE HOLY SPIRIT

The Greek word *charisma* that defines "gift" comes from the root word char, meaning "a gift of grace, a free gift, divine gratuity, and spiritual endowment." Judging from the meaning of charisma, one may safely conclude spiritual gifts are free will gifts of grace emanating from the Holy Spirit's desire. We refer to some Christians as charismatic, identifying such persons as having one or more of the nine gifts functioning in their lives. However, this assumption is not entirely true especially as charismatic Christians do not in general exercise supernatural gifts. All sorts of reasons may be given for the lack of spiritual gifts in our regular church services or in practice in the lives of believers. But we need no longer occupy ourselves with excuses; instead, the Body of Christ should pull on strengths and work with possibilities. Our communities are crying out for messengers of hope.

But the manifestation of the Spirit is given to each one for the profit of all (1 Corinthians 12:7).

TO MANIFEST IS TO DISPLAY

Each gift in operation is a manifestation and display of the Holy Spirit in a believer's life. Spiritual gifts serve to evidence the Spirit's activity in our lives. Several scriptures confirm the indwelling presence of the Holy Spirit in a born-again believer in Christ Jesus. It makes sense for the resident of a home to have times of outdoor indulgence. The Holy Spirit is God inside of us; His gifts reveal His awesomeness in mere mortals.[207] With so much immorality and permissiveness challenging our societies, the Church is the only hope of salvation of men, women, and children. More needs to be done in the area of evangelism, especially prophetic evangelism. Greater levels of formal education, technological advancement, and communication explosion leave the Church with no choice other than an overhaul of strategies to fulfill the mandate to the world. Youth prophetic programs need to be structured strategically with the aim to speak destiny into our young people who are more in touch with society than most in Christian leadership. The time has come to mobilize the entire army of God, to activate all spiritual gifts for the sake of the unsaved in our communities.

Corporate Benefit

There is corporate benefit to the Body of Christ when believers are encouraged to exercise spiritual gifts as the New Testament model confirms. The pride of the 21st century is being exhibited through antichrist legislation, with particular reference to Britain. Trained legal practitioners in the Church need to be incorporated in leadership activities for wisdom's sake. Although we are not to covert contentions, it is wise to remind oneself that the days are evil. When challenges arise, either from or against, the Church has to offer qualified responses to diffuse controversies.

As mentioned previously, spiritual gifts have been given to the Body of Christ for the profit of all. In other words the display of spiritual gifts enhances members of the Church and beneficiaries of outward ministry. If the function of prophecy outlined in detail in later chapters is to be interpreted in relation to the overriding call to evangelize then it can be said that only a healthy Body is able to translate good news to the dark world. Training in spiritual gifts management and application is extremely important especially in the present diversities of cultures in our societies. An important aspect of the prophetic involves the ability to understand changing times and trends like the children of Issachar (1 Chron. 12:32).

Interpret the Times

Our society makeup is so much more different from when apostle Paul wrote to Christians in Corinth. Many cities in the Western world are cosmopolitan while Christian missionaries are from diverse cultures.

Cultural paradigms call for interpretation, so that general language of love for articulation of the heart of God is adopted by the Church. A divided army cannot fight effectively. We face fierce competition for the souls of men from occultic, satanic, and new age sources who seek to exalt themselves against the knowledge of God.[208]. Another reason for training in accurate application of spiritual gifts hinges on negating the effect of immature practice of spiritual gifts on many leaders. If we get it right in the house, the chances are that we get it right outside. The message on my heart expressed through this book revolves around getting every professed believer active in practical ministry. I also wish to highlight the need to recognize varying degrees or levels of spiritual empowerment for the sake of accountability. If Christ set some apart to equip others for the work of ministry then attention ought to be paid to the obvious distinction referred to in Ephesians chapter 4:11.

You Have a Gift!

As each one has received a gift, minister it to one another as good stewards of the manifold grace of God (1 Peter 4:10).

Every believer has been endowed with a gift and the Bible encourages usage of such for the benefit of others. We are to be good stewards of spiritual gifts. A good steward is a good manager, a good administrator of valuables entrusted in their hands. The Greek word *oikonomos,* defining steward, comes from two words *oikos* meaning "house," and *nemo* meaning "to arrange." As believers are activated and functional in the gifts, they become good "house arrangers." With skilled organizers, the house of God works to full capacity overflowing into street activities—and relevance.

Stewardship duties require believers to pay due diligence to the ways gifts are applied. Stewardship involves responsibility and as we read in Scripture such duty is to the multi-dimensional grace of God. The idea of managing God's grace requires a measure of accountability. *Polupoikilos,* the Greek word that defines *manifold,* comes from two words, *polus* meaning "much" and *poikilos* meaning "varied, many colored." In effect each gift in manifestation is a revelation of the multi-dimensional nature of God. Unless the entire army of God is released to fulfill its divine mission, the Church limits her access to many facets and expressions of God in ministry.

NINE GIFTS MENTIONED IN FIRST CORINTHIANS 12

Although this writing focuses primarily on the gift of prophecy it is important to examine, albeit by way of minor exposition, other spiritual gifts for broader response. There is need to encourage wider spiritual gift usage in our daily lives. The key of gift operation is in purpose and vision. Until the Church embraces the call to the harvest field of Christ, our passion for spiritual empowerment may be inspired by carnality. Many believers today are only interested in learning about prophecy. But prophecy is only one of nine gifts of the Holy Spirit, and prophet one of five offices mentioned in Ephesians 4:11. So important are the lives of the lost that Jesus, in His teaching on principles for city taking, insisted that any person whose agenda was not in sync with His agenda to gather the lost, *"scatters abroad"* (Matt. 12:30).

Apostle Paul did not diminish the importance of the other eight gifts but was responding to the culture of the church in Corinth at the time addressing underlying problems. The present Church needs to function in line with the Lord's prophetic clock, interpret the times, and operate proactively to save the nations from further chaos. A culmination of spiritual gifts bestowed on the Body by the Father, Christ, and the Holy Spirit along with the Word of God leaves us with no excuses.

CATEGORY 1 — *Revelation Gifts*

In this section I shall draw inference from the ministry of Jesus Christ in attempt to interpret spiritual gifts in practice for the sake of present-day application. It is important to bear in mind that the gifts of the Holy Spirit were not given until after the Spirit's outpouring.

The named spiritual gifts in this category reveal issues not previously known by the bearer of the gift.

1. WORD OF WISDOM

This gift in manifestation is the Holy Spirit's granting of prudence, understanding, or direction about what to do in a given situation. A typical example would be the case of the tax collectors who plotted against Jesus seeking to entrap Him by His words. After prefacing a tricky question with words of exaltation they asked, *"Tell us, therefore, what do you think? Is it lawful to pay taxes to Caesar, or not?"* Using word of wisdom, Jesus perceived their wickedness, and said, *"Why do you test Me, you hypocrites?"* (Matt. 22:17-18).

Word of wisdom operates also as a supernatural sense of direction—to know God's perspective in a given situation. In application, word of wisdom may enable a practitioner to receive divine strategy for accomplishing God's will in a given situation. Jesus had the Holy Spirit without measure and therefore walked continuously in divine wisdom (John 3:34). He also applied word of wisdom in the incident of the woman accused of adultery in John 8:1-12. The scribes and Pharisees were *"testing Him, that they might have something of which to accuse Him."* This case portrays the value word of wisdom can bring to world evangelism especially in Islamic nations where awkward questioning may require supernatural responses.

2. WORD OF KNOWLEDGE

The gift of word of knowledge is also known as message of knowledge. This gift in manifestation reveals the divine will and plan of God supernaturally. Also a person operating in the gift of word of knowledge is able to receive divine information pertaining to a person or an event that would not otherwise be known. A classic example in the Bible is the case of Elisha and the king of Syria. Elisha received, by supernatural means, information concerning the king's war plans against Israel supernaturally. By alerting the king of Israel, Elisha foiled Syria's war plans, to this effect the king of Syria questioned, *"Will you not show me which of us is for the king of Israel?"* (2 Kings 6:1-12). The Church needs to deploy this potent gift, especially in spiritual warfare projects. Elisha was simply conveying details of spiritual espionage. I have never been part of a spiritual mapping group or team but I found a few years ago that the more I prayed for my city, the more I was taken in the spirit and shown areas of historical and spiritual significance.

Word of knowledge also offers believers knowledge of mysteries of the Gospel hidden in prophecies, types, and shadows and history of the Old Testament. Prophetic apostles, prophets, preachers, pastors, and teachers tend to flow in this gift especially when bringing divine truth into present-day application.

Word of knowledge can be useful in counseling situations to uncover and unveil previously concealed unrighteousness that works against deliverance from bondage. This aspect of word of knowledge reveals its nature as a valuable freewill gift for pastoral benefits.

Jesus also functioned in the gift of word of knowledge when He identified the donkey He was to ride into Jerusalem. He knew supernaturally which donkey and exactly where it was tied. (Matt. 21:1-9; Luke 19). Although a prophet, again Jesus was stating facts known supernaturally because the donkey was already tied waiting to be loosed. In the case of the Samaritan woman, Jesus exercised prophecy when He revealed His eternal nature as "Living Water" truth that is progressive in revelation (John 4:9-18). However, when He revealed her past life He used word of knowledge to reveal details of her life previously known to her and those familiar to her. To this she responded, *"Sir, I perceive that You are a prophet"* (John 4:19).

The Church must not lay unnecessary emphasis or become parochial about the order in which gifts apply; but training enables practitioners to broaden their expectations.

3. DISCERNING OF SPIRITS

This gift endows believers with supernatural ability to discern the spiritual realm, especially the true source of power professed by a Christian. The gift of discerning of spirits enables true discernment of motives of persons professing Christ. It assists the church in discerning evil spirits in operation in people's lives—even believers. The gift of discerning of spirits in operation will enable the Church to receive and understand plans of the devil and his cohorts. To establish effective counteraction to the enemy's plans, supernatural understanding of the routes through which the devil launches his attacks must be deciphered. In wider application this gift can also help discern true or false prophets as in the case of Elymas, the sorcerer of Paphos, who withstood Barnabas and Paul's mission to the proconsul (see Acts 13:4-12). The gift of discerning of spirits can come in handy when praying for the sick to know the true source of their illness. At times we default into blaming the devil for most illness; however, true Holy Spirit-inspired discernment may save on precious time for medical treatment, and invite the power of another gift—gifts of healings.

HOW TO OPERATE THE REVELATION GIFTS

True belief in the supremacy of God the Father, God the Son, and God the Holy Spirit will prepare a believer to function out of a natural mind-set. God resists the proud (1 Pet. 5:5). Apostle Paul exhorted his spiritual son Timothy to, "Stir up the gift of God which is in you through the laying on of my hands" (2 Tim. 1:6).

Sphere of Application for Revelation Gifts

These gifts may be used at all times in everyday activities. The revelatory gifts are extremely effective in evangelism, especially during casual encounters with strangers who do not expect personal circumstances to be revealed in a way only the Lord is able to expose. I once met a lady at a nail studio who was on her way to a psychic after suffering recent bereavement of her father. A bereavement counselor at the hospital where her father died gave her contact information for a psychic. I asked her if she would come along to church if I prayed to the Lord to reveal the answers she was seeking. Then I prayed with her. To my delight, the Lord answered, revealing details known only to a person who could have been close family. The psychic lost a client that afternoon. The owner of the nail studio, herself a Christian, informed me a few weeks later that the lady had attended several Christian events since our meeting. My experience confirms the value word of knowledge in practice would add to outdoor ministry.

CATEGORY 2 — *Power Gifts*

4. FAITH

Faith as a gift of the Holy Spirit offers supernatural ability to believe the Lord implicitly. This supernatural gift exhibits a God-endowed ability to respond to adverse circumstances with implicit hope and trust in the word of God[209] I feel particularly drawn to this definition for the way it helps me communicate my personal experience. Faith was the first supernatural gift I received from the Holy Spirit in 1992, when at the beginning of my professional course to train as a solicitor my first son was diagnosed with atypical autism.

The early church functioned in tremendous faith through imprisonment, stoning, and beating to proclaim the Gospel of the Kingdom. The apostles specifically operated in supernatural faith in confronting entrenched ideologies, divination, and witchcraft. Old Testament types may be employed in interpreting gift of faith in our present time. Daniel was operating in the supernatural dimension of faith when he trusted God whose name he chose to worship to save his life in the den of lions (see Dan. 6:16-23). David trusted the covenant God of Israel to give him victory over the giant, Goliath (see 1 Sam. 17). Samson also supernaturally slew 1,000 Philistines with the jawbone of a donkey (see Judges 15:15). They all exhibited courage beyond natural ability to save their dignity and, in David's case, that of his nation.

Sphere of Application for Faith

Gift of faith is to be exercised as a matter of course, especially in times of prayer and intercession through difficult times. Faith is practiced in the ordinary things of life; in our everyday living we exercise faith by simply believing God through our words and actions.

5. WORKING OF MIRACLES

This is the manifestation of divine power beyond the ordinary. This gift manifests as the divine enablement to perform acts that could not be done naturally. It also works closely with faith and gift of healings to bring supernatural releasing authority over bondages, strongholds, sin, and sicknesses. Jesus Christ is the *Dunamite*, meaning the miracle worker. History records supernatural exploits through the ministries of Smith Wigglesworth, Kathryn Kuhlman, Maria Woodworth Etter, and more recently Kenneth Hagin. Servants of God like Benny Hinn, Rheinhard Bonnke, and Kenneth Copeland, and many others are currently being used in the working of miracles to set free the captives.

6. GIFTS OF HEALINGS

This gift is applied to numerous diseases and cases of sickness of which believers have been given supernatural ability to bring healings and deliverance to others.[210] The use of plural "gifts" and "healings" creates the impression of duplicity, but in actual fact "gifts of healings" refer to the distinct anointing available to the Body of Christ for healing specific illnesses such as distinct anointing for cancer. I attended a church where the pastor moved in distinct anointing for healing cancer.

CATEGORY 3 — *Vocal Gifts*

As the name suggests, the gifts in this category inspire supernatural utterance.

7. PROPHECY

The gift of prophecy refers to supernatural prompting of the Holy Spirit to declare the mind of Christ as revealed. Prophecy involves hearing what God is saying and declaring the same.[211] At a foundational level prophecy is for congregational edification, exhortation, and comfort.[212] Every Spirit filled believer may manifest or function in this supernatural gift as the Spirit wills.[213] The Word of God is prophecy in itself as John stated in the Book of Revelation (see Rev. 22), and so God may speak to a person through His written word. Prophecy serves as an effective tool in evangelism.

Sphere of Application for Prophecy

Prophecy may be used at prayer times, church services, and counseling sessions. Prophecy, if used accurately, wisely, and in order with protocol of the office, will be invaluable as a tool of evangelism.

8. Different Kinds of Tongues

This gift avails a born-again believer the supernatural ability to speak in new tongues not learned naturally. I attended a church in England for many years, where my then-pastor, David Carr would at times, during prayer meetings in particular, speak in native Indian tongues. On one occasion a visitor to the church recognized his native Indian language and understood the divine messages.[214] Praying in unknown tongues helps our prayer time as we connect with the Holy Spirit, who in turn processes our prayers appropriately.[215] Apostle Paul approved of tongues as prayer language, however his teachings encouraged interpretation especially in congregation settings.[216] Jesus also spoke of signs that would follow believers in Him, which include to *"speak with new tongues"* (Mark 16:17). Praying with the Holy Spirit means praying in tongues unknown to the speaker but given by the Holy Spirit. The Scripture encourages the use of both when praying—our understanding (familiar language) and our heavenly language.[217]

Sphere of Application for Gift of Tongues

The gift of tongues is encouraged during church services if there is someone to interpret. However speaking in tongues during evangelism should be discouraged since the purpose is to convert souls and not confuse issues.

9. Interpretation of Tongues

The gift of interpretation of tongues is the supernatural ability to interpret spiritual tongues described in the previous section. A person who speaks in tongues may also ask the Lord for interpretation of the tongues prayed. It is important to note the interpretation of tongues is not a work of natural translation or the ability of a translator but is a supernatural declaration of divinely inspired words not known to the speaker.

Sphere of Application for Interpretation of Tongues

Following apostle Paul's teachings, tongues—when used in congregational services— ought to be followed by interpretation for edification of the listeners. It is important to remember that all nine gifts of the

Holy Spirit are freewill gifts available to every born-again believer. To maximize potential of these gifts in practical ministry, training is important. More than one gift may be in operation at a time but the most important thing is to conceive a supernatural mind-set for the sake of the Kingdom of God in the lives of the lost.

Chapter Nine

GIFT OF PROPHECY

Aim: To examine the gift of prophecy in greater detail.

Webster's dictionary defines *prophecy* as, "Prediction of the future under the influence of divine guidance; act or practice of a prophet; something predicted."

Some within the Church believe prophecy and prophets were a part of the early church age and as such bear no relevance in our time. Quite often the same people agree with the presence of pastors, teachers, and evangelists in the Church today. Prophecy is an ongoing manifestation of God's voice through the church age until the coming of the Lord. Believers in Christ Jesus remain the only channels for transmitting God's voice on the earth. The Spirit and the Bride must say with one voice: *"Come"* (Rev. 22:17).

I personally have a problem with people claiming to speak on behalf of the Lord as prophets who do not appreciate the need to become a functioning member of a local church assembly.[218] Prophets who are to "equip" should themselves be accountable to some other recognized leadership. No matter the state of the church, or the purported spiritual maturity of a prophet or prophetic believer, there is still a place for submission. I am not calling for the abusive, Saul-type control of some church leadership. A true prophet should understand the power generated from honoring Saul until God's appointed time.[219] Isolated or generalized cases of spiritual abuse cannot be used as reason for absentia from corporate worship.

The gift of prophecy in believers in our time needs to mature into a new dimension of manifestation.[220] Prophecy in the mouth of believers should mature beyond comforting other believers into outright demonstration of the Spirit and power on our streets.

The presence of prophecy is recorded throughout Bible history,[221] with every dispensation birthing new expressions of the prophetic gift.

PROPHECY IN THE OLD TESTAMENT

In the Old Testament prophets served as the voice of God in the nation, speaking exclusively for the Lord and hearing assuredly from the Lord.[222] False prophets also existed in Israel even though the offense of false prophesying attracted punishment by stoning.[223]

The Hebrew word *Nabi*, generally used to define "prophet," means "one who proclaims, announces, declares, utters communications, a spokesman, a heralder." Another Hebrew word, *Ro'eh*, means "Seer" and is used to define the role of the prophet. Both functions of the Old Testament prophet—as spokesman and as seer—are captured in the narrative of Saul and his father's lost sheep in First Samuel 9. In the discussion of gratuities to be taken to the prophet for insight, the Bible relates:

> *Formerly in Israel, when a man went to inquire of God, he spoke thus: "Come, let us go to the seer"; for he who is now called a prophet was formerly called a seer* (1 Samuel 9:9).

The prophets were called seers to describe God's medium of communication. I fail to see any benefit in distinguishing the two functions of seer and prophet. Neither Ephesians 2:20 nor Ephesians 4:11 distinguishes the function of a seer from a prophet. However, I have often believed in having prophetic roundtables with grouping established along distinctive anointing. For instance, some prophets are particularly gifted in time-specific prophecies, a rare gift that needs to be multiplied in the Body of Christ, while some hear through dreams. Nations and churches will benefit more from specific gifts tasked in hearing God in line with their distinctive anointing. I believe such gatherings will achieve greater accuracy in shorter periods of meetings. My service in the prophetic ministry revolves around both functions of seer and prophet, with my particular distinctive in timing and dates. However, my motivation remains in the service of the Lord.

GOD'S REPRESENTATIVES

Prophets in the Old Testament represented God by speaking under the power of their mantle like Elijah[224] and as moved by the Spirit of God.[225] The Scriptures show prophets as people who maintained close relationship with God that enabled for free flow of supernatural utterance. Prophets led their lives separated unto the Lord. They stood in the inner counsel of God in order to reveal His mind to His people.[226] Kings honored God Almighty through His prophets.[227] The time of Malachi saw the end of an era of prophets, as did prophet Samuel who symbolized the end of the time of the judges. For 400 years Israel lived without the voice of God.[228] Malachi spoke of the coming of Messiah and His final coming with final judgment and vindication for the righteous.[229] Again, the prophetic ministry received a dramatic change to its shape and form in the birth of the New Testament church. The most significant change came in the outpouring of God's Spirit *"upon all flesh"* instead of the lone prophet *nabi* or seer *ro'eh*, or the watchman *chozeh* or *shamar* who stood before God and spoke for God to his people.[230]

GIFT OF PROPHECY IN THE NEW TESTAMENT

The outpouring of God's Spirit saw "all flesh" gifted with spiritual gifts including prophecy.[231] Prophecy in the New Testament is a gift of grace, hence we are to be wise stewards of the Lord's manifold grace of God.[232] Prophets, being beneficiaries of the new covenant in the blood of Jesus, are still required to speak with accuracy. Although prophets are no longer stoned alive for getting prophetic words wrong, the responsibility for accurate prophetic utterance is still critical. The Scriptures encourage testing and weighing of prophecy, but we are not to despise prophecy.[233] The Greek word *propheteuo* which defines prophecy means: "to foretell events, divine, speak under inspiration, exercise the prophetic office, to proclaim a divine revelation, to prophesy, to foretell the future; to speak forth by divine inspiration, to break forth under sudden impulse in lofty discourse or in praise of divine counsels."

Greek *prophetes* defines the function, and signifies a person who speaks for another, in this case, God. The New Testament definition of prophet reveals two functions of the prophetic as *predictive* or *interpretative*. This is the call I make to the Body of Christ to assume more of an interpretative role in relation to the world we have been commissioned. As said, prophecy has been given to the Church as a freewill gift. Christ also gave some to be prophets, to nurture and equip the saints for outward ministry. Any person called by Christ in an equipping function mentioned in Ephesians 4:11 to his body serves the Lord by training his army in the knowledge of Christ.

The gift of prophecy is mentioned in a cluster twice in the Bible alongside other spiritual gifts and gifts in persons given by Christ to the Church outlined in Ephesians 4:11 to facilitate the two mentions I refer to. These mentions need to be examined to elucidate a way forward for the Church as a prophetic community in 21st century impact. In an age of information technology explosion, with increase of education and awareness, the Body of Christ needs to operate in ongoing supernatural insight into world affairs. Greater levels of literacy mean more people are engaging in intelligent discussions and are also more poised to engage in energy-sapping debates. For these reasons the prophetic church would be wise to deploy all spiritual gifts to counter the agenda of the antichrist. We are not to conform to this world but as God's children, believers are to be transformed by having our minds renewed.[234] The mind is renewed through daily revelation of God's awesomeness.[235] Corporate and individual evangelism initiatives will become more strategic if powered by insight into a listener's life, delivered with gentleness and wisdom.

Many people across spheres of society are disillusioned—seeking to fill voids in their lives. Psychics remain in business serving people's feelings of emptiness, an unfortunate side effect of civilization. The significance of predictive prophecy cannot be overemphasized; however this function of prophecy has left the Church a selfish body concerned only for personal breakthrough. We have a generation of Christians whose ears have been trained to receive personal prophecy with little guidance about how to fulfill the commission of Christ. This trend needs to change if we are to engage with the heart of Christ which is for the unsaved who seek answers to questions.

The fact of divination surrounding our governments cannot be dismissed as modern-day indulgence. Paul and Silas faced the same challenges to the Gospel being received by the proconsul (Acts 13:4-12). The most important responsibility of the Church today centers on a concept I have termed "out-letting" the prophetic. We are to release grace of our supernatural gifts on the needy in the same manner as Peter and John *"at the gate of temple which is called Beautiful."*[236] The Church needs to re-engage with the gift of prophecy as an outdoor evangelistic gift as well as an inspirational gift for congregational worship.

Roman's 12 — Categorization

Having then gifts differing according to the grace that is given to us, let us use them; if prophecy, let us in prophesy proportion to our faith (Romans 12:6).

Apostle Paul's teaching to the Roman church about spiritual gifts also mentioned prophecy. A study of prophecy in the New Testament would be incomplete without examining Paul's intentions in categorizing this gift twice—once in Corinth and again in Rome. Generally, two approaches are taken by biblicists to this mention. One view is to adopt all the spiritual gifts in this category as an extension of all other gifts mentioned in the New Testament. The spiritual gifts mentioned in Romans 12 are prophecy, ministry, teaching, exhorter, givers, leadership, and mercy (verses 6-8). The implication of seeing the Romans mention of prophecy as an extension of the Corinthians mention of the same gift would be far-reaching for the Church. If that were the case apostle Paul would have made provision in his teaching for a whole new structure for operating prophecy or at least expanded his teaching beyond the mention as it stands in that Scripture. Imagine stopping in the middle of giving a prophetic word to a stranger or as part of church service to check pre-learned notes, or consult the mind memory bank to find out whether to exercise First Corinthians 12 gift of prophecy or Romans 12 gift of prophecy.

The second opinion views prophecy in Romans 12 as an overlap of Paul's teaching in Corinth (see 1 Cor. 12:12-29) and Ephesus (see Eph. 4:11). My humble submission would be in line with the understanding of mention of prophecy in Romans 12 as an overlap of other mentions of prophecy as a New Testament gift to the Church to be exercised through believers. Both mentions relate to the same important gift of prophecy. I do not believe the intention was to compartmentalize or for categorization, but on the contrary the aim was to establish firm doctrinal foundation for effective practice of spiritual gifts at the time. The Church ought to be preoccupied with achieving clear prophetic sounds in the nations,[237] so the lost can hear the voice of God through His sheep who know Him.

Paul was fulfilling his call to the Gentiles by spreading the Gospel, and equipping the converts to serve as converters of souls themselves. Spiritual gift mention and teaching in the churches was to address doctrinal imbalances for the sake of effective ministry. Beyond correcting wrong practices, Paul was equipping the Church to minister to one another and then to the wider constituency of their communities (see 1 Cor. 12:3). He pointed out that, *"We, being many, are one body in Christ, and individually members of one another"* (Rom. 12:5).

God who created the heavens and the earth has formed each of His children to be unique individuals. God spoke to Jeremiah on the occasion of his commission to prophetic ministry to reveal Jeremiah's uniqueness (see Jer. 1:5). Thus each believer is blessed with spiritual gifts such as prophecy (see Rom. 12:4). Uniqueness manifests in believers through the varied gifts: *"as God has dealt to each one a measure of faith"* (Rom. 12:3).

1 Corinthians 12—Categorization

Prophecy in 1 Corinthians, as mentioned previously, is one of nine gifts given to the body of Christ by the Holy Spirit for the profit of all. Application of prophecy requires proactive partnership with the Holy Spirit who is the giver and dispenser of the gift. The Bible encourages, *"But earnestly desire the best gifts"* (1 Cor. 12:31), confirming proactivity and not passivity on the part of would-be prophesiers. Prophecy is presently largely contained within the Christian experience unlike in the early church that saw prophecy practiced predominantly outside of buildings (see Acts 11:27-30; Acts 21:8-14).

The early church in the Book of Acts exercised prophecy for the furtherance of the Kingdom of God (see Acts 13:1-4; 15:22). The Holy Spirit's power fell upon believers to catapult their ministries from local to national and international status, making them *"witnesses to me in Jerusalem, and in all Judea, and Samaria, and to the end of the earth"* (Acts 1:8).

Certain fundamental aspects of this profoundly significant gift have already been covered in previous chapters. But the clarion call to the Church remains—to relocate the gift of prophecy to street activities. The time has come for prophetic engagement; a time that the Church is required to embrace the Issachar Mandate with fresh impetus for prophetic evangelism.

Chapter Ten

◄━━ ☰◆☰ ━━►

PROPHECY — STILL RELEVANT TODAY

Aim: Announce the clarion call to the prophetic church.

Pursue love, and desire spiritual gifts but especially that you may prophesy (1 Corinthians 14:1).

Within reason the gift of prophecy may be exercised as and when necessary, to stir up, uplift, and comfort other believers.[238] It is important for those who operate spiritual gifts such as prophecy to do so with utmost wisdom. The desire for the gift of prophecy should proceed from compassion for the unsaved. Prophecy is to be received as an effective tool for evangelism. The Church is required to appreciate the value prophecy brings to Christian activities in our time and its potential, if used accurately, in the marketplace. The present need of the Church is to seek to understand the times we live in, and to interpret the times. Accurate analysis of signs of the times is bound to stir up believers with urgency to put our supernatural gifts to effective use.[239] An important aspect of the work of the Holy Spirit, the Giver of gifts, is to awaken the Church into present truth (Luke 3:22). One may conclude the Spirit of God comes to overhaul the Church's activities and

119

to bring us up to speed with Heaven's pace.[240] Unless our hearts are in tune with that of Father in Heaven, our natural eyes will conveniently shut out the pain in our world.[241] Unless the compassion of Jesus Christ outflows from the Church to the poverty in our world we do not deserve the manifestation of His power. Spiritual gifts are available to the Church to enable her to represent Jesus Christ as a "solution center." We represent a people who may not have all the answers to the world's problems, but who do have answers to some problems. At present the church has not assumed that corporate mantle of "Watchman" to nations (Ezek. 33:2).

Your Gift Counts!

As each one has received a gift, minister it to one another, as good stewards of the manifold grace of God (1 Peter 4:10).

Jack Deere, commenting on First Peter 4:10, writes, "The Holy Spirit has sovereignly given spiritual gifts to every believer in the Body of Christ so that we may better serve one another."[242] The biggest problem the Church will encounter in the present apostolic dispensation will come from ill-trained Christian soldiers or worse still, untrained soldiers. Unless believers are properly equipped to manage the supernatural opportunities to minister the Gospel at previously inaccessible spheres, we may run into difficulties. Muslims in Islamic nations are crying out for the delivering power of Jesus Christ. Many nations of the Western world have themselves become missions fields by rejecting the laws of God and attracting evil of our day.

Mike Bickle summed up potential vitality the Church is able to mobilize at all levels of life in his book. "I believe there are people with prophetic giftings resident in most cities of the earth where the Church is being established. They may be immature, but they are probably present."[243] This is the army I speak for—who must be mobilized and equipped for divine assignments. There is a lot of preaching that *informs* believers of their destiny and calling but not enough assistance is provided when it comes to helping the same people *discover* their destiny.

I grew up under the same false hope preached aloud but was fortunate to have been brought under the wings of the Holy Spirit who I met after reading Benny Hinn's book, *Good Morning Holy Spirit*. Men preached about freedom but held on to the keys that opened gates of spiritual maturity. Preaching to believers about unattainable spiritual freedom leads to greater captivity than clear-cut hierarchical control. It is the truth that makes us free.[244] The time has come to equip the saints for the work of the ministry. Our focus should be centered on fulfilling the great commission to *"preach the gospel to every creature"* (Mark 16:15).

Prophecy is not an exclusively oratory gift. Present-day operation of the gift of prophecy needs to expand beyond speech. In the Old Testament dispensation, prophecy was conveyed through symbolism and allegories. Prophets slept on their sides to identify with national sin and bore the burden of nations as Isaiah regularly did (see Ezek. 4). The unspoken world of creative arts, dance, drama, painting, and music (such as heard in Rick Joyner's Morning Star band) provide some of the choices being suggested. As it is said, "a picture paints a thousand words." God speaks to His children within levels of maturity. He speaks to reveal His heart to us as His children and His disciples on the earth. According to First Corinthians 14:1, every believer is to desire the gift of prophecy.

Zeloo, a Greek word that defines "desire" means "to be zealous for, to burn with desire, to pursue ardently, to desire eagerly or intensely." Spiritual gifts should be pursued zealously for the sake of reaching the hearts of the unsaved. Apostle Paul did not want the Church ignorant of the importance of spiritual gifts. He also did not want them to be found lacking in supernatural abilities: *"So that you come short in no gift, eagerly waiting for the revelation of our Lord Jesus Christ"* (1 Cor. 1:7). Prophecy is not an end but a means to an end.

A LESSON FOR THE LOCAL CHURCH

The church is an initial training ground for prophetic ministries. Jesus Christ announced His prophetic ministry in a synagogue, also quoting the word of a past prophet, Isaiah.[245] The prophet's calling is to primarily serve as trainers to the prophetic church community. To this extent prophets should serve as part of a local church structure and in their fivefold function.[246] A resident prophet in a local church assembly, discussed in later chapters, should be recognized as part of the leadership team to help establish order for the practice of prophecy in a church. The church then serves as an apostolic or sending base for prophetic believers who desire to use prophecy especially for evangelism. I would like to lend support from a case study in examining protocol of prophecy in church services in the present dispensation.

Important points to bear in mind:

1. The gift of prophecy is available to all believers (1 Cor. 14:31).

2. Not all believers are prophets (1 Cor. 12:28, Eph. 4:11).

3. You do not have to be a prophet to exercise the gift of prophecy (1 Cor. 14:1).

4. The difference in the gift and office is in responsibility of the role/function of the prophet. One is a gift and the other a function/office requiring greater level of accountability for managing another's future (1 Cor. 12:4-10; Eph. 4:11-16).

CASE STUDY

Linda decides to visit Kings Church one Sunday morning on the invitation of her friend, Lucy. During the worship time, Linda suddenly felt an urge to prophesy. As the pastor was about to speak Linda declared aloud, *"The Lord says to you, 'Rejoice, again I say rejoice,' the Lord is calling you all to rejoice. He wants you to respond in worship."* This time raising her voice she said, *"The Lord says rejoice; He wants you to respond in your worship."*

What is your discernment of Linda's actions? Several issues are raised in Linda's case study. It would be worth giving some of those issues consideration.

Observations: Should Linda have spoken out at Kings Church?

Since Linda was only visiting Kings Church she ought to have inquired of Lucy, a member of the church, the protocol for operating spiritual gifts. Linda could also have asked for a leader and written down whatever she felt the Lord was laying on her heart. Churches generally operate on guidelines for spiritual gifts use (see 1 Cor. 14:40). In this case, Linda's message fits the description of inspirational prophecy or foundational level prophecy within First Corinthians 14:3. Although the word may have been inspired from the Holy Spirit, the fact remains that Linda's chosen method and timing of delivery exposes her immaturity and lack of training (see 1 Cor. 14:32). The content of the word would be received as encouraging by most members but her status is likely to cause confusion because she is not a member of the church (see 1 Cor. 14:33).

Kings Church should be seen as a training ground for Linda's future ministry and a place where the first lessons on protocol of prophetic ministry would be learned. Linda's destination is to the cosmopolitan societies of the 21st century with people who are waiting to hear the message of the Gospel. She also needs to learn the lesson of wisdom. As Paul taught, prophecy when exercised in a church service is for exhortation, edification, and comfort to all. It is important to ascertain whether members of Kings Church were stirred up, built up, and comforted. A so-called prophetic word blurted out by a stranger in the middle of a church service telling the congregation to be joyous may not be well-received. Linda appears to have taken over the service, drawing attention to herself. The attitude she exhibited is often common in immature prophetic persons.

Recommendations: Linda should be gently called to one side and corrected—preferably by a female prophet. With the level of disruption she may have caused to usual church routine, a male leader could present an intimidating figure. The leadership of Kings Church should discreetly suggest to Linda to give her prophecy in full after the service. The leader should then steer the service back into familiar order. To openly disagree with Linda's declarations may throw the members into further confusion and unease.

Questions: Did the Lord give permission to Linda to speak?

Honesty and transparency in the heart of a prophesier will produce seeds of humility. The Bible so rightly warns: *"The heart is deceitful above all things, and desperately wicked; who can know it?"* (Jer. 17:9). It is important to discern the motives of the heart. At all times in congregational prophecy, there must be approval from the leadership of the church, who may need to also test for false prophets.[247]

Is order being established?

A fundamental protocol of prophecy in congregational worship would be devalued by permitting random utterances. A zealous believer that Linda presents is required to match purported zeal with divine wisdom. After all, she would be expected to honor rules of conversation in the secular world by not interrupting the flow of a conversation she did not initiate. In the Kings Church case, Linda, not being a member, may be accused of interrupting a flow of divine communication with Heaven that began with worship. It is crucial to observe a key principle laid by apostle Paul's teaching on prophecy to the Corinthians. He said, *"Even so you, since you are zealous for spiritual gifts, let it be for the edification of the church that you seek to excel"* (1 Cor. 14:12).

Linda's utterances may have been tolerated by the worshipers had there been a formal introduction of her ministry by a pastor or leader before she prophesied. But instead she clearly interrupted the course of service.[248] Remember, prophecy is for the edification of the church body, in this case it is not clear if the church was edified. Her words are perfectly scriptural but she seemed to have chosen the wrong time to prophesy. The Word of the Lord spoken in time accomplishes intended divine purpose of God. God's Word is like a hammer that breaks rocks into pieces.[249]

The desire to exercise the gift of prophecy, whether in or outside of the gathered church experience, must be founded on righteous motivation. Linda's judgment of her environment (visitor to Kings Church) and timing for delivery of the prophecy (middle of worship) could have emerged from a wrong heart attitude and motive. Linda is not necessarily a false prophet but because she was not instructed by the Holy Spirit to speak when she did, she opens herself to criticism for her action. In other words, lack of wisdom may be harmful to a genuine prophetic person.

Past hurts, rejection, wounding, and other adverse personal circumstances could affect a genuine prophetic ministry.

STUDY CONSIDERATIONS

In the example of Linda's prophecy, several reasons may also be deduced from Linda's actions.

As stated, the Holy Spirit may have allowed the error of practice to create opportunity for Linda to learn and mature (see 2 Pet. 1:20-21). If this were the case, she may humbly receive rebuke from the elders of the church if a breach of the code of practice in supernatural gifts in that local assembly is pointed out to her (see 1 Cor. 14:31-33).

Every church ought to have standard guidelines about operating spiritual gifts (see 1 Cor. 14:40).

Linda's prophetic utterance may have been inspired by a fleshly desire to draw attention to herself. This would be at variance with the Holy Spirit (see Gal. 5:16).

Linda may have felt the need to be recognized as a prophetic voice (see Gal. 5:20). However, *timing is extremely important.*

Pray that the Holy Spirit will reveal the time to speak and inspire you to speak.

Investigate the protocol for operation of supernatural gifts if in a church setting— especially if you are a visitor to that assembly.

Outside of church (in the marketplace, community, etc.) apply wisdom especially when witnessing to people of other faiths. The Bible urges us to *pursue love zealously.*

Discern inspiration and purpose for prophetic words given. Every prophecy must line up with the Word of God (see 1 Pet. 1:19-21).

Chapter Eleven

━┄━ ☰◈☰ ┄━

GIFT OR OFFICE?

Aim: To emphasize the difference in responsibility between a prophetic Christian and the office function of Prophet.

IDENTIFYING A PROPHET

Over the years as I have read and studied apostle Paul's teaching in Ephesians chapter 4 regarding a group of designated functions in believers in Christ, I have been left with a burden to pray. My prayers have been for those who are called specifically for the task of *"equipping the saints"* in the way Paul challenges. Further reading of Ephesians chapter 2 about the practical outworking of the anointing on two of the five functions—apostles and prophets—reveals the fundamental responsibility of the two gifts for building a healthy church. My simple mind cannot comprehend reasons for the disparity between the teachings of apostle Paul and the practice in our present-day church.

The saints are to enjoy a twofold benefit package—to equip the saints for the work of the ministry and for the edifying of the Body of Christ.[250] The responsibilities of all five functions toward the saints

127

are clearly outlined with timing specified.[251] However, the Church has been run largely by only two of the five offices—pastors and teachers. Ephesians 2 welcomes believing Gentiles as *"members of the household of God,"*[252] and recognizes their substance, *"having been built on the foundation of the apostles and prophets, Jesus Christ Himself being the chief cornerstone."*[253]

A clear objective may be deduced from the text in Ephesians 2:21-22 and Ephesians 4:13-16—to see a mature Church established and fulfilling her mandate on the earth. The prophetic call for the equipping of the saints should incorporate an understanding of who is to equip. It is important for the prophetic community to identify those who are to train others in the gift. In other words we need to be armed with enough teaching to identify our trainers. This responsibility cannot be entirely relegated to the gift of discernment but practical, logical, sound biblical teaching will help believers identify true from false prophets. When a person is registered for a training course, the tutors are introduced according to their particular subject specialty. Students are not just thrown into a classroom with the teachers, given the recommended textbooks, and told, "We're all the same so let's learn!" Ephesians 4 specifies a category of people in the Body of Christ with particular gift ability to be used for the maturing of the saints. The reason the saints need to be equipped is so their destiny as disciples of all the nations—to heal and to cast out demons, among other things—is fulfilled. The success of the saints for Christ-ordained mission is referred to as "edifying of the saints." To edify is to stir up. Revelation 12:11 also refers indirectly to the saints being stirred up when testimonies of overcomers by the blood of Jesus are shared.

There is a fine line of separation that defines a hierarchy rather than categorizing an important group whose commitment to duty will see the Church in her rightful position.

My People Perish for Lack of Knowledge

As previously mentioned, Jesus Christ bridged gaps in time by fulfilling prophecies that pointed to His coming. He bridged gaps in understanding also by patiently expounding important principles of life. Jesus was prepared to be controversial in His handling of some issues of injustice.[254] With the gift of prophecy, Jesus converted the soul of the Samaritan woman in a time when Jews shunned the Samaritans. I believe the Church in our time is being called to "arise" with urgency to bring clarity in aspects of our faith that leave even our members in confusion. Again, it is important for the prophets in our midst to clearly define guidelines for identifying prophets, thereby ensuring accountability and responsibility bearing. The Lord brought a charge to Israel through the prophet Hosea, saying, *"There is no truth or mercy or knowledge of God in the land"* (Hos. 4:1). Israel was rejected by God for rejecting knowledge, and warned also: *"My people are destroyed for lack of knowledge"*[255] (Hos. 4:6). Several scriptures warn of the antichrist agenda, the existence of many antichrists, teachers of fables, and false doctrines. Although the Bible is a closed book and sufficient for all our needs,[256] in truth, believers of our time, especially those in some parts of the Western world, ignore the demand of the Spirit to take heed of the Word of God.

A dangerous trend I have observed in young prophetic ministries is a dependence on "pictures" as a means of communicating revelation but without Scripture base. Prophetic impressions, pictures, and symbolism are all used to convey prophetic messages; however, the dependence I refer to appears to come as a result of lack of exposure to other equally potent expressions such as visions and trances as in the early church. It is dangerous for believers in modern-day societies not to study the Word of God.[257] We must emulate the believers in Berea who confirmed spiritual hearing with the Word of God.[258] There is now a desperate need to bridge gaps in understanding, for instance the identity of a prophet, functions of prophets, and responsibility of prophets to the Church and nations.[259] Clarity births understanding and understanding gives knowledge.[260]

AMOS MANDATE

The Church has been under pressure from secular lobbyists with antichrist agendas, influencing governments in Europe and the U.S.A. For instance, some so-called Christians who choose the gay lifestyle want the Bible re-written to suit their lifestyle choice. We need to embrace the *"Amos mandate"*—*becoming burden bearers for the Lord.* Burden bearing is a higher level of intercession when some people may be called upon to carry the weight of the need of the Lord, sometimes showing signs of identification with the need on their physical bodies. Prophet Amos said:

> *"I was no prophet, nor was I a son of a prophet, but I was a sheepbreeder, and a tender of sycamore fruit. Then...the Lord said to me, 'Go, prophesy to My people Israel'"* (Amos 7:14-15).

My personal burden is to see greater cohesion and cooperation in the functioning of the responsibilities of prophets as a matter of duty. Prophets are not to be seen as celebrities, but as servant-leaders that they are. Prophets function in a high calling of God with amazing responsibility to God and His people.[261] How does a "youngish" believer with a distinct leadership calling recognize a fivefold function or responsibility on their life? How does the rest of the church accept this youngish believer as "prophet to the nations" unless their gifting can be attested to by people who ought to know?

It is my strong belief that unless a consensus blueprint is produced by a group of recognized, experienced prophets, the task of identifying prophets will remain daunting. The Body of Christ will benefit from such a document that represents a work of collaboration that helps identify specific gifts.[262] It is important for such a document to take into cognizance the diverse streams of the prophetic. A broad-based document with information from identified prophetic streams and their distinctive will make an invaluable training tool. The Body of Christ needs to work toward achieving the order and decency of worship proposed by apostle Paul in his teachings to the church in Corinth.[263]

Pastors have often been criticized for not recognizing prophets and prophetic persons. But should a pastor who has to solve the problems of a thousand members once a week in a one-hour speech be burdened with the responsibility of identifying prophets and prophetic people? Today's pastors spend most of the week counseling believers who choose not to study the Word of God, believers ignorant about how to receive freedom and liberty offered by the blood of Jesus. These pastors simply do not have the time to perform litmus tests on alleged prophetic ministries.

An important aspect of the fivefold responsibility of prophets includes assisting the rest of the Church in identifying who the fivefold servant leaders are. The Church has benefited from excellent studies, writings, and teachings about prophets and prophetic ministries from great men such as C. Peter Wagner and Bill Hamon. Now we need more of such ministries if a well-equipped army is to be grown for these last days.[264] Stewardship responsibilities of prophets must encompass assisting the Body through sound teaching to identify prophets.

Most fivefold office servants desire to fulfill the call of God on their lives but would benefit also from a corporate house cleaning. It is hardly believable looking at some churches today that the Bible described the Church as the house of God, *"the pillar and ground of the truth"* (1 Tim. 3:15). The Church cannot possibly "house" truth unless we honor truth. Being prophetically engaged and the Issachar Mandate require the Church to understand the times and to know what people ought to do. If the Church is to be the pillar of truth in our 21st century existence it must stand righteous before God and man. If the Church is the pillar and ground of truth then we must wear truth as our overalls. The world is desperate to interpret spiritual truth through the lives of children of the living God. Christians are the Bibles many people have to read. Unless the saints are activated, the prophets have no one to equip for the work of the ministry. Proper training in the use of the prophetic gift serves to close the gap between prophets and prophetic saints.

THE SAME BUT DIFFERENT

What differences exist, if any, between a prophet and any other prophetic Christian who exercises gift of prophecy?

What the Bible says concerning gift of prophecy: *"There are diversities of gifts, but the same Spirit"* (1 Cor. 12:4). The Body of Christ has been endowed with diversities of supernatural abilities to effect the commission of Christ on the earth. Believers in Christ Jesus are encouraged to desire prophecy but not at the expense of pursuing love. Apostle Paul declared, *"And though I have the gift of prophecy, and understand all mysteries and all knowledge, and though I have all faith, so that I could remove mountains, but have not love, I am nothing"* (1 Cor. 13:2).

What the Bible says concerning office of prophet: *"And He Himself gave some to be apostles, some prophets, some evangelists, and some pastors and teachers"* (Eph. 4:11).

Only Holy Spirit-filled believers in Jesus may prophesy, but not all are prophets according to the cited Scripture. The gift of prophecy can be manifested by every believer, including those used in the office function of prophet. But the Bible cautions those who would use the gift to do so in *"proportion to our faith"* (Rom. 12:6). Believers have varying degrees of faith levels with every level capable of kick-starting the gift of prophecy. Maturity here refers to God-given spiritual maturity—not the number of years in prophetic ministry.

I believe that by virtue of inherent responsibilities outlined in the Ephesians 4 mantle, prophets are gifted with the necessary maturity to serve as God's messengers even in our time. The level of responsibility or seriousness of the messages entrusted to a prophet over a number of years that establish a track record should be seen as an indication of their spiritual maturity. I am suggesting that spiritual maturity should be weighed from Heaven downward rather than from earthly perspectives. Apart from the mention of Philip's four virgin daughters[265] in the New Testament suggesting natural age, in no other instance is enough mentioned to infer the age of apostles and prophets. Philip's daughters cannot be seen as a reliable authority in weighing spiritual maturity, even though I make a mention of them, because they may have been virgins from choice. The Old Testament gives credence to my argument that regardless of age, prophets even in our time are gifted, especially for the function with which God set them apart in the first place. Moses,[266] Gideon (Judges 6:15), Daniel,[267] and Jeremiah[268] were young and each faced issues of inadequacy when commissioned, but God assured them of His enabling presence and power. According to Scriptures[269] prophets have been given to the Church by Christ for specific duty to equip. As said, prophets as members of the Body of Christ also have the indwelling presence of the Holy Spirit and are able to manifest gift of prophecy. However, an added responsibility is embedded in the prophets' mandate: *"For the equipping of the saints for the work of ministry, for the edifying of the body of Christ"* (Eph. 4:12).

The heart of the Father is that every child of God receives spiritual equipping, enabling them to function in their own particular calling and mission. The Church should primarily concern herself with the sole purpose for which spiritual gifts were given, otherwise we will keep going round in circles. Prophets need to get on with the task of training believers to use their prophetic gift effectively. The call of the prophet goes beyond training and equipping to include serving as Watchman for the Lord—to the Church and nation, to warn of danger. The residing anointing in individual prophets determines the focus of their ministry, so for instance a prophet particularly gifted in timing operates on an Issachar-type mantle. A modern-day role of prophets that I perceive as unavoidable as we prepare for the return of the Lord will be to pronounce judgment. Prophets of our time will speak of mercy but then assist the Church in interpreting judgment.

THE OFFICE FUNCTION OF PROPHET

As emphasized previously, the prophets, along with other categories of responsibilities mentioned in Ephesians 4, are to "equip" the Body of Christ for the work of the ministry. The Greek word *katartismos* defines equipping as "making fit, preparing, training, perfecting, and making fully qualified for service." Katartismos is used in classical language for setting a bone during surgery, implying, therefore, that the training of saints has the same effect as the proceeding wholeness after a bone has been mended in a body. "Making fit for service" implies disjointing or misalignment of a tool that prevents a unit of machinery from functioning at its maximum potential. With the Body of Christ still in need of equipping, one can assume that we have functioned as a disjointed and misaligned body.

133

For example, an English law governing sale of goods (Sale of Goods Acts 1979 - SOGA) implies certain terms into a contract of sale known as conditions. Goods supplied under contracts of sale must correspond with their contractual description. Contractual goods must be fit for the particular purpose for which, with the knowledge of the seller, they were bought. Even if the buyer does not expressly make known the purpose for which the goods in question were being bought, the law requires such goods to be fit for all the purposes for which such goods are commonly used. The goods must correspond with the sample, if the order made was sample-based, or in some cases samples and description.

A consumer who purchases a steam iron may return it to a retailer if every time it is used on clothes they become creased instead of straightened. The steam iron would be rejected as "not fit for its purpose" under the consumer law regulations. Natural laws as in SOGA 1979 are promulgated to vigorously protect consumers and stringent measures taken to ensure high standards from manufacturers.

The members of the Body of Christ are retailers of the Gospel and are expected to perform in the same manner. The Gospel, if preached as we have been commanded,[270] will work on our behalf for the purposes for which it was given,[271] *for sake of the lost.* We are to demonstrate the power of God—to move in power.[272] We cannot afford to disappoint the creation who eagerly waits for the release of the equipped saints who will in turn release them.[273] We are Christ's ambassadors. Our lives must therefore mirror image the life of Jesus. We must be about "our Father's business"[274], healing the sick[275], raising the dead[276], feeding the multitudes[277], praying[278], and teaching the flock[279]. We have been given the important task of preaching the Gospel to all creatures[280] and making disciples of all nations.[281] The time has come to embrace the priorities accordingly.

EQUIPPING THE SAINTS

The fivefold servant-leader's duty in the corporate responsibility of the Church following the katartismos definition of *"equipping"* is *"to make every member of the body of Christ fit for service, relevant in the kingdom of God activities."* The Blood of Jesus guarantees every believer a place in the corporate enterprise of the Church.[282] The need to equip will not diminish, *"Till we all come to the unity of the faith and of the knowledge of the Son of God, to a perfect man, to the measure of the stature of the fullness of Christ"* (Eph. 4:13).

The importance of an informed army cannot be over emphasized:

> *That we should no longer be children, tossed to and fro and carried about with every wind of doctrine, by the trickery of men, in the cunning craftiness of deceitful plotting, but, speaking the truth in love, may grow up in all things into Him who is the head—Christ* (Ephesians 4:14-15).

The relevance of each member needs to be clearly communicated:

> *From whom the whole body, joined and knit together by what every joint supplies, according to the effective working by which every part does its share, causes growth of the body for the edifying of itself in love* (Ephesians 4:16).

CHRIST—THE FULLNESS OF THE GODHEAD

All the power and fullness of the Godhead has been given to the Body of Christ in order to usher the Church into all that God intends her to be. The Church as the visible expression of Christ on the earth must walk in her destiny and purpose.

Purpose of the Fivefold Ministry:

1. Perfecting or maturing of saints.

2. For the work of the ministry.

3. For the edifying of the Body of Christ.

Five is God's number for grace and also for responsibility, confirming much of my argument in this chapter. The Tabernacle of Moses had five bars which held the entire structure together as one tabernacle, a model for the present day fivefold ministry to the Church (Exod. 36:31-34). To maximize potential, the Ephesians 4:11 fivefold function of apostle, prophet, evangelist, pastors, and teachers needs to be fully restored to the

Church. Once more the prophet stands in a leadership role in the government of the Church as an appointee of Christ.

The role of the prophet is often described as an office, distinguishing the responsibility from the Holy Spirit gift of prophecy to the Church as a Body. *The office of the prophet is a leadership-headship function. In proper administration, the office of prophet represents Christ's servant-leadership role as prophet in His lifetime.* This means that the manifestations of Christ's ministry as prophet ought to be visible in the prophet's office today. Following the pattern set by our Lord Jesus, today's prophets should do greater works than Jesus, the apostles, and Saint John.[283]

Jesus served as prophet in His lifetime.[284] It was in this capacity that He affirmed and confirmed John the Baptist's prophetic ministry. Jesus fulfilled the fivefold function as follows:

◆ He challenged false doctrines, religion, and tradition. He performed miracles with signs and wonders following (Apostle).

◆ He reached out to the Samaritan woman, an untouchable in society, to convert her soul and that of her community (Evangelist).

◆ He often spoke of appointed "times" and also predicted His death (Prophet).

◆ He was moved by compassion for the people and referred to people as: *"My sheep hear My voice."* He fed 5,000 people at one event (Pastor).

◆ He regularly taught lifestyle principles through parables (Teacher).

IMPORTANT POINTS FROM EPHESIANS 4:11-16

The fivefold function has been set apart for the ongoing process of equipping the saints until:

1. Maturity is attained (verse 14).

2. False doctrines are challenged (verse 14).

3. All manner of deceit is identified and challenged at every level and walk of life (verse 14).

4. Saints speak/proclaim truth in love (verse 15).

5. Deliverance from lies brings transformation and saints can live their lives (verse 14).

6. Saints find common ground in their differences (verse 16).

7. Saints become effective in their unique callings (verse 16).

8. Ensuing growth of the entire Body of Christ is released into personal gifting (verse 16).

These points, according to the Bible, would result in numerical growth, *"causes growth of the body,"* and lead to internal strengthening of the Body of Christ, *"edifying of itself in love"* (verse 16).

Prophets, along with other leadership functions mentioned in Ephesians 4, are in our midst today and must be affirmed (see Romans 12).

Chapter Twelve

⊶ ≢♦≣ ⊷

SPHERES OF INFLUENCE

Aim: To emphasize the impact of spiritual gifts in spheres of society.

Apostle Paul taught extensively about the value of prophecy in the congregational setting; however, prophecy, as with other spiritual gifts, are not limited to formal church services. Since being taught the subject of spheres of influence in early 2004 by the Holy Spirit, I have been inspired by the revelations therein. Although fundamental to fivefold functions, especially office of apostle, I have chosen to extend with benefit of revelation this vital truth. My motivation comes from the fact that every believer is apostolic,[285] although not all are called to be apostles. *Apostle* means "sent one." An understanding of spiritual boundaries is extremely important if we are to achieve the responsibilities of the Great Commission in an evil day.

Apostle Paul said: *"We, however, will not boast beyond measure, but within the limits of the sphere which God appointed us—a sphere which especially includes you"* (2 Cor. 10:13).

139

Paul spoke of his authority within a spiritual territory. He spoke of a designated sphere that included humans—the believers in Corinth. Again, I seek to challenge and motivate further teaching on spheres of influence, or territories of impact, beyond its relevance to apostles. My objective is to encourage all believers in Jesus to embrace the world we have been commissioned to change. Consider a person who is flying to an island resort vacation. Do they ask themselves—do I have the authority or not to visit this place? The passionate, attention-to-detail plans with which vacations or holidays are usually organized do not, to my mind, reveal people in fear of their destination. Why then should believers, who have been given permanent, reusable tickets by the blood of Jesus to any land in earth suffer from phobia of the outdoors? Why do we prefer the comfort of our modern edifices while people around us go to hell? Apostle Paul boasted within his sphere because he recognized he had a territory of impact. Paul said, *"For even if I should boast somewhat more about our authority, which the Lord gave us for edification and not for your destruction, I shall not be ashamed"* (2 Cor. 10:8).

The words of his commissioning revealed his sphere, the group of people he was being sent to share the Gospel with (see Acts 9:15). Born-again believers also have spheres (see Acts 17:26). Believers are apostolic by the commissioning words of Mark 16:15 *"Go into all the world"* and Matthew 28:19, *"Go therefore."* To *go* means "to travel, to change location, to move, to embark on a journey." *Sent* means "to be directed, to follow an order, to be assigned, to be commissioned." The Greek word *apostoleo* means "sent one." Believers are apostolic people who need to be conscious of spiritual climates of the territories where they are held accountable by God.[286] Apostles bear the authority of their Sender (Matt. 28:18).

RECOGNIZING YOUR TERRITORY OF CALLING

Paul was writing to the church in Corinth at the time concerning those who challenged his apostolic authority, some even perceiving him weak. Some thought him only bold as an apostle when he wrote letters (see 2 Cor. 10:9-11). It would appear from Paul's statement in defense of his ministry that a child of God, whether an apostle or not, needs to recognize their spiritual territory or area of calling. A believer enjoys more of God's blessing within their divinely appointed sphere of impact and influence. God's grace rests abundantly and demonic activities are heightened also in such areas.[287] Although demonic activities also appear fiercest in a person's designated area of impact, greater levels of grace result. This is apparent from the fact that the God who calls is also the God who empowers His apostolic agents.[288]

INTERPRETING SPHERES OF INFLUENCE

For the apostolic church to destroy, demolish, and dethrone demonic operations in an area, the prophetic gift must be fully deployed in partnership with apostolic grace against the forces of darkness. A more fundamental factor is the equipping of the saints in understanding of corporate and personal spheres of influence. So, for example, when a pastor announces a "prayer walking" program to the church, every person who participates comes under the corporate sphere of such a pastor. The city of planting is the sphere of influence of the church as a body, and God's grace protects and guides the members under the elected spiritual leadership of the pastor. Also, with regard to city-taking initiatives, the church in the area must first ensure that the congregation receives understanding of the corporate commission of the church to the city.

It is important also for the believers to be encouraged to apply their individual authority as new creation believers (Phil. 4:13). Believers may use their authority to evangelize (Mark 16:17). However when stepping into a wider scope of spiritual authority such as city taking, it becomes necessary to come under a corporate identity with a clear line of leadership guidance. A prayer walking initiative, for instance, should accomplish its objective if the principles laid down in the leadership guidelines are followed.

FIRST APOSTLES

The pastor in the example may function as an apostle even though he does not bear the title "apostle" as a prefix to his name (1 Cor. 12:28). That pastor has a sphere of influence as an apostle to the city beyond his church. He can then lead an army to war. In his capacity and fivefold function as apostle a more defined sphere is understood according to apostle Paul's teaching. God is a God of order. Understanding spiritual boundaries limits the number of casualties in any spiritual warfare. Pastors and believers avoid out of time war. If the Church is to fulfill her apostolic mandate, the need to understand the revelation of spheres of influence cannot be overestimated.

A person whose spiritual authority is regional will make the most impact in the particular region of their calling. Such a region becomes their spiritual territory and their sphere of influence. Should this person then decide to conduct spiritual activities outside of the designated region, into a national sphere for instance, they may experience resistance from invincible demonic forces. There is no harm in conducting spiritual matters wherever a believer desires; however, the aim of this teaching is to emphasis the importance of understanding spiritual boundaries and functioning effectively within such boundaries. Any extension beyond the obvious sphere of calling must only be embarked on as a result of a clear leading of the Lord.

"THE WORLD IS MY PULPIT" — JOHN WESLEY

The time has come for believers in Jesus Christ to operate in John Wesley's conquering, apostolic mind-set. Apostolic people are sent people; they are messengers and can only fulfill destiny while mobile—not trapped in buildings observing ceremonial doctrines while the world beyond perishes. We are the Lord's messengers and today the authority of the Church is being challenged by lack of results to back up the words we preach. Christianity has been much challenged in the 21st century by humanism, secularism, Islam, and several other philosophical persuasions. But the Church's role in society is not to battle false ideology using physical, natural weapons (see 2 Cor. 10:3-4). We war by being the power house of deliverance, healing, and hope we were created to be. Paul was a man commissioned to a particular group of people within society.[289] He had a sphere of influence as an apostle.

THE AUTHORITY LIES IN THE MANTLE

Apostle Paul's commission: *"But the Lord said to him, 'Go, for he is a chosen vessel of Mine to bear My name before Gentiles, Kings, and the children of Israel'"* (Acts 9:15).

Paul was raised for a specific purpose. By implication, Paul's teaching on spheres of influence in Second Corinthians 10 was already spoken within the commissioning words of his ministry. The words, "Gentiles, kings, and the children of Israel," clearly define his territory of calling. It defines the area where he must achieve the purpose of his calling and where he must be tested most. The Jews opposed Paul in Corinth (see Acts 18:5-6). Repositioning his mind Paul said, *"From now on I will go to the Gentiles."* This statement appears to suggest he had inadvertently limited himself up to then by teaching only the Jews in Corinth. He was operating outside of his primary location of calling. Opposition comes when we confine or limit the anointing of God on our lives to a territory outside of our calling or when the need to move to the next level arises and we miss it. When Paul made up his mind to go to the Gentiles, his ministry took another turn. Verse 8 reveals, *"The ruler of the synagogue, believed on the Lord with all his household."* Others in the city believed also and were baptized.

Like the example of Elijah and the widow, God's provision becomes more apparent when we embrace our spheres of influence.[290] The supernatural power with which activities of the demonic are confronted and defeated are most potent in a person's sphere of influence.[291] A believer naturally feels more able to fight opposition in a place of calling as a matter of ownership.[292] Recognizing a sphere arms a person with the necessary confidence to war against spiritual forces that often challenge our destinies.[293] Spiritual opposition within a person's sphere serves as God ordained stepping stones for the next level of accomplishment.[294]

When Paul stepped into his purpose (not that teaching the Jews as in Acts 18:5-6 was not within his purpose, as we see from Scripture that he did teach Jews) divine favor dealt a blow to demonic opposition. The Lord spoke, *"Do not be afraid, but speak, and do not keep silent; for I*

143

am with you, and no one will attack you to hurt you; for I have many people in this city" (Acts 18:9-10).

DO NOT OVER-EXTEND!

Paul's message is to be taken seriously today. Wherever the Lord commissions a believer to task, His manifest provision is activated by obedience to cause. Many intercessors I have met suffer from over-extension of spiritual authority within a sphere of influence, and have met with 'out of time wars'. Apostle Paul explained, *"For we are not overextending ourselves (as though our authority did not extend to you), for it was to you that we came with the gospel of Christ"* (2 Cor. 10:14). God has pre-gifted his children with supernatural abilities to respond to societal needs. In other words we are God's "Rapid Respond Squad" on the earth. The boundaries of our dwelling have been predetermined, so each child of God is relevant in their community (see Acts 17:26). Believers should not, therefore, clone one another's vision or cause hindrances to another's purpose. Prophetic engagement calls for the release to assignment of the unique supernatural abilities within each believer. I know of churches whose visions change in line with personal agendas of some in leadership positions. Churches will be planted regularly to accommodate expected converts if we were truly expecting to fulfill the commission of Christ. Believers preach and sing so much about revivals but once a family member opens up a storehouse for the "preached about," and "sung about" revival, all hell breaks loose. So, what exactly is the Church asking for?

One may run the risk of over-extending designated spiritual authority if lessons on spiritual boundaries are not imbided. A well-meaning child of God may attract unnecessary spiritual warfare if taken into battle without proper protection or covering of a leader envisioned for battle. The case of angel Gabriel,[295] who encountered resistance from the Prince of Persia, and then anticipated further resistance from the Prince of Greece[296] provides an example of the existence of spiritual territories and boundaries. Other examples in the Bible include the case of Diana the goddess at Ephesus[297] and Elymas of Paphos[298]. A child of God, commissioned as Paul was for instance in Ephesus, acts within their sphere of authority when engaging in spiritual warfare, deliverance, worship, or other activities that aim to preach the Gospel of the good news in the area specified. But in the case of the seven sons of Sceva, they were not endowed with the same spiritual authority in Ephesus as they attempted to "clone" Paul's anointing.[299] He taught, *"And so I have made it my aim to preach the gospel, not where Christ was named, lest I should build on another man's foundation"* (Rom. 15:20). Apostle Paul's words should be received as a matter of protocol for self-seeking ministries. Paul was committed to *"the gospel for the uncircumcised,"* while Peter was committed to *"the gospel for the circumcised"* (Gal. 2:7). The Church must respond to the call of Jesus Christ for more laborers rather than compete over a bit of the vineyard. The harvest is truly plentiful!

Apostolic Mandate of Fivefold Functions

It is important to note once more that the Ephesians 4:11 fivefold office functions bear defined spheres of authority. I was called to move my ministry activities to the city of Birmingham in England through a dramatic vision in 1998. I was shown a dark graveyard with dark mist descending. Five men in black anoraks, or overcoats, stood guard over the graves. An old church stood in the graveyard cutting an image of a city under siege. Interestingly, five apostles of prayer had kept the fire of intercession burning from this city with a call to the Church to "Pray For Revival". They withstood the five strongmen who guarded the city under siege by the spirits of death. With this vision came a message to lay down the work I was involved in—organizing prayer conferences in London which had reached a peak by this time in 1998. Due to the intense fear, I felt the Lord gave me a strategy with which to enter the city. He spoke to me about a city square that was a "source" of power—negative and positive. To overcome fear from the strongman over this city I was to fast and pray for one month (February 1999). The Lord taught me to prophetically position myself at the square every morning. I had never visited the square, and was not even sure it existed apart from the instructions I had from the Lord.

To break the power of fear that gripped me I was to declare the Lordship of Jesus over Birmingham. I prayed and fasted for 28 days. During that time I was invited to a Church in Oxford and given a message of "possessing the gate of the enemy" on the last day of my fast. The couple accompanying me knew where the square in Birmingham was located; the place of spiritual power. They took me there and as I stood in Centennial Square I confronted the spirit of fear. Four months later whilst attending a prayer gathering I had the privilege of receiving prayers and blessing from some of the city prayer leaders I referred to. Birmingham became a sphere of influence within a nation of my assignment.

Five years into facilitating national prayer from my base in Birmingham, the Lord revealed the "King Kong" spirit as the strongman over the city. Shortly afterward, the Lord declared the city gates opened. I was led to prophesy that Joyce Meyer and Benny Hinn would visit the city. A few hours later, on a Sunday, an e-mail from Joyce Meyer ministries confirmed the Word of the Lord. A conference was planned for Joyce Meyer and my ministry was to assist along with others. When Joyce handed me a bouquet of flowers she was presented with at a preconference meeting, I interpreted that gesture as a prophetic sign from the Lord that indeed the gates of the city of Birmingham had been opened. This experience was repeated a few months later as the organizers of a Benny Hinn conference made contact, once more confirming the Lord's concern for cities, nations, and continents.

INTERNATIONAL SPHERES OF AUTHORITY

The case of Jeremiah is an example when international authority was bestowed on a fivefold prophet.[300] Compare Jeremiah's international ministry to Amos' regional commission. Amaziah the priest of Bethel challenging Amos said, *"Go, you seer; flee to the land of Judah. There eat bread, and there prophesy. But never again prophesy at Bethel for it is the king's sanctuary, and it is the royal residence"* (Amos 7:12-13). Amaziah sought to contain Amos' anointing to Judah, Amos' homeland. But Amos was sent to Bethel by the Lord and commissioned to prophesy to *"the people of Israel."* Although Amos was sent to Israel; the high priest wanted him out of the strategic place of the "King's sanctuary," center of power, and place of authority. But Amos insisted on obeying his calling: *"And the Lord said to me, 'Go, prophesy to My people Israel'"* (Amos 7:15).

Paul was commissioned to the "Gentiles, kings, and also the children of Israel" to reach them with the Gospel of the Kingdom. He encountered contentions to his authority both from humans and from invincible spiritual beings within his sphere of influence. Paul went on to point out the importance of not engaging in spiritual warfare with carnal, fleshly weapons (see 2 Cor. 10:3-6). Spiritual wars are fought with God-empowered weapons to demolish all spiritual forces employed against the will of God for His children. The devices of the enemy are channeled toward frustrating attempts at accomplishing divine tasks within a sphere of authority. Paul as an apostle wore the mantle of his office with the necessary authority to enable him to function as an apostle. Functioning in clear understanding of his assignment and boundaries, Paul established divine order in the churches planted.

The time has come for the Body of Christ to embrace corporately Christ's heart for cities and nations. Unless our hearts beat in rhythm with the heart of Jesus Christ, the Church will remain weakened by division and competition. To be relevant in a sphere of influence the church must become salt and light (Matt. 5:13-14). We must apply spiritual gifts in our walk and sphere of application to demolish forces that challenge the will of God in the lives of people we are meant to reach—those *"whose minds the god of this age has blinded, who do not believe, lest the light of the gospel of the glory of Christ, who is the image of God, should shine on them"* (2 Cor. 4:4).

PROMOTION

Promotion comes within a person's sphere of influence. Paul said, *"Not boasting of things beyond measure, that is, in other men's labors, but having hope, that as your faith is increased, we shall be greatly enlarged by you in our sphere"* (2 Cor. 10:15).

He boasted only in his own accomplishments through Christ. Paul said, *"For I will not dare speak of any of those things which Christ has not accomplished through me, in word and deed, to make the Gentiles obedient"* (Rom. 15:18). Paul's statement from verse 15 may be summarized in the following unwritten principles of practical ministry:

1. Boast in the accomplishment of your designated divine task only.

2. Do not become a stumbling block to others' spiritual work by boasting in "other men's labor."

3. Faithfulness to spheres of influence produces spiritual growth and faith of those we commit our anointing to mentor.

4. Leaders are advanced through their spiritual children.

Paul made clear his mission: *"To preach the gospel in the regions beyond you, and not to boast in another man's sphere of accomplishment"* (2 Cor. 10:16). While fulfilling the mandate of God upon his life, Paul was aware of certain dynamics necessary for the success of his mission. Paul's statement from verse 16 may be summarized in the following unwritten principles of practical ministry.

Paul implied:

1) He would not place limitations on his ministry *(to preach the Gospel in the regions beyond you)*.

2) He would not encroach on others' ministry assignments but would honor and affirm the work of others within a sphere of influence *(not to boast in another man's sphere of accomplishment)*.

It is vital that those who manifest spiritual gifts are armed with an understanding of spiritual boundaries in order to avoid spiritual warfare. Acting in excess of authority and territorial influence attracts out of time wars. As God's chosen channel for divine communication of His multifaceted wisdom, every member of the Body of Christ has the entire earth as our sphere of influence (see Ps. 24:1). John Wesley said, *"The world is my parish."* We have a responsibility to reach a wider constituency of people on the earth *"beyond you,"* as Paul warned the church in Corinth. Our mandate is to *"make disciples of all the nations"* (Matt. 28:19), and to *"preach the gospel to every creature"* (Mark 16:15).

Chapter Thirteen

┄┄ ≖◈≖ ┄┄

FUNCTIONS OF PROPHECY

Aim: To emphasize the intrinsic advantage prophecy adds to
formal congregational services, its effectiveness as a tool
of ministry, especially in marketplace and community
evangelism.

Function means "purpose, meaning, role, task." The purpose of
this chapter is to examine the functions identified in the Bible of
prophecy. My aim is to challenge believers through evidence provided
to covet the gift of prophecy (1 Cor. 12:31, 14:1), and to boldly use it,
with wisdom. The purpose of prophecy is so richly defined in First
Corinthians 14:3. Paul stated, *"But he who prophesies speaks edification and exhortation and comfort to men."*

THREE FUNCTIONS MENTIONED IN 1 CORINTHIAN 14:3

Edification

To *edify* means "to build up, instruct, benefit, uplift, and to
enlighten." Following this definition, prophecy when spoken has the
effect of uplifting the hearer, inspiring, and building confidence where the

151

individual has faced discouragement.[301] Prophecy, due to its revelatory nature, also has the capacity to instruct a believer. Prophecy avails the hearer of clarity and direction in areas of Scripture interpretation where confusion may have existed. Revelation of God's heart awakens the spirit of the hearer with hope for present and future breakthrough. The benefits ensuing from mature exercise of the gift of prophecy are encapsulated in the definition of the word *"to edify."* People are inspired by functionality and results achieved.

Exhortation

To *exhort* is "to urge, advise, caution, admonish, recommend, or warn." Prophetic words have been known to redirect from harm to safety depending on the nature of the message they bear. The potency and weight of this supernatural gift are evident from the definition of its functions outlined, hence love must underpin prophecy (see 1 Cor. 14:3). Prophetic words may contain instructions to a hearer that could cause discomfort; however, such words must be weighed against the nature and character of God (see Jer. 9:23-24). So a prophesier may be required by God to give a word of rebuke, although this is more common with the office of prophet. No matter the circumstance being addressed, love must be displayed. Every child of God is expected to speak kindly, peaceably, and humbly to all men. Prophecy at the foundational level fulfills the First Corinthians 14:3 responsibilities. The Word of the Lord brings direction and instruction to any person poised to listen. God's Word must reflect who He is, and must not be condemning, controlling, or judgmental.

Comfort

To *comfort* is "to soothe, reassure, bring cheer, bring a feeling of relief from pain or anxiety, lessen one's grief or distress, and is to give strength and hope by means of kindness and thoughtful attention." Prophecy must reflect God's character and heart.[302] A prophet with a national mandate is responsible to declare the mind of Christ to that nation (Amos 3:8). To fulfill the requirement for weighing prophetic words, prophets should belong to networks or roundtables of mutual submission and accountability where words are put to corporate weighing against the written Word of God. Prophecies so weighed should then be communicated to the Church with suggested strategy for application. Prophetic words must comfort those who are addressed. God cannot speak outside of His nature or outside of His character. Any words spoken in the name of the Lord that affect listeners adversely, leaving listeners anxious, agitated, and bewildered, should be rejected. When prophecy speaks a message of rebuke, love must flow from the heart of the prophet who delivers the word. God chastens those He loves.[303]

STRATEGY

One of the most vital functions of prophecy is the release of strategy. Divine insight gives birth to godly strategy.[304] A revealing of God's heart opens doors to divine breakthrough. God is Messiah the Breaker, the One who establishes His people in their destiny path.[305] The Bible reminds us of the consequences upon God's people of not being armed with strategy.[306] An organization that is not linked with its commissioning body functions without authority of accreditation. Unless the Church is able to read God's prophetic clock, we run the risk of skirting the same mountains (see Deut. 2:3). God was saddened by Israel's spiritual impotence caused through sin and rebellion: *"Therefore My people have gone into captivity, because they have no knowledge..."* (Isa. 5:13).

The Church in present times, as was the case for Israel, will need divine strategy to achieve corporate breakthrough in cities, for instance: *"My people are destroyed for lack of knowledge"* (Hos. 4:6). Knowledge here refers to knowledge of the mind of God revealed through His Word.

When God's people lacked revelation in Old Testament times, rebellion and lawlessness took over. In times of apostasy the hearts of the Israelites became vulnerable to idolatry; while in idol worshiping they lost sight of God's commandments. During such times in the Old Testament spiritual darkness engulfed Israel, and prophets pronounced the mind of God. Sin in any land still separates the people from the Lord's manifest presence and voice. Israel's cycle of rebellion, sin, and repentance cast prophets in a role dramatically different from our time. One example of this role of prophets is captured in the bible account of the Midianite attack on Israel in the Book of Judges. God sent a prophet to Israel to remind her of her disobedience before he commissioned Gideon as a deliverer. In this case the prophetic was not justifying God's action but interpreting the times so Israel could learn from her mistakes. As a result of their sin, Israel suffered judgment by the hands of wicked Midianites. Despite their disobedience, God's heart was still to bring Israel out of judgment and into her deliverance (see Judges 6:8). The prophetic church in our time needs to interpret the end-time signs to alleviate the problems of a confused world. As the prophetic Bride of Christ pursues unbroken fellowship with Him, He in turn will reveal the depths of His heart to His body.

EFFECTIVE SPIRITUAL WARFARE

Prophetic sight enables the Church to pray effectively and strategically. Knowing the mind of God through His revealed will generates confidence in a praying Christian (Jer. 29:11). With benefit of supernatural insight into the subject of intercession or prayer petition, an intercessor will be more disposed to effective and fervent praying. God urges His children to partner with Him.[307]

The Hebrew word *qara* which translates "call" means, "to call out to someone, cry out, address someone." *Qara* is often used to describe "calling out loudly in order to get someone's attention."

To achieve effectiveness in prayer, especially spiritual warfare, the Body of Christ must learn to partner with God. In recent times, the world has enjoyed greater harvest of apostolic and prophetic prayer strategies pioneered by internationally-recognized ministries. Spiritual gates of many nations previously closed by demonic ideologies and ancient foundations of iniquity are now open to recognized evangelists like Benny Hinn, Rheinhard Bonnke, and others. Nevertheless, the Body of Christ owes a lot to the pioneering work of apostles of prayer such as C. Peter Wagner and Larry Lee. I remember many years ago when Larry

Lee visited as a regular guest speaker at one of London's greatest charismatic events—Mission to London—organized by Morris Cerrullo Ministries. His pioneering teaching impacted many people, including myself.

Prophets and prophetic intercessors such as Cindy Jacobs (USA), Rod and Julie Anderson (UK), and John Mulinde (Uganda) have been used to unlock destinies of numerous cities and nations. Bold prayer and reconciliation initiatives have been recorded in Heaven for redemption of our nations. One such reconciliation event was organized in Berlin in 2005 by Roger Mitchell of Passion UK, Dr. Segun Johnson, Micheal Schiffman, Samuel Rhein, and Chris Seaton with others from African and European nations. The event was to redress the effects of colonialism that caused Africa to be carved up like a wild hunt by the European nations.[308] Prophetic intercessors have been known to discern, perceive, and then declare the mind of God over whole cities in confrontation with demonic principalities. The importance of prophecy in spiritual warfare is highlighted through Paul's charge to his spiritual son. Paul said, *"According to the prophecies previously made concerning you, that by them, you may wage the good warfare"* (1 Tim. 1:18).

Timothy was being urged to wage informed warfare against false doctrine permeating Ephesus. He was to wage the good warfare with the revealed Word of the Lord spoken into his destiny at his ordination. Beyond prophecy, believers should earnestly desire supernatural living. Spiritual gifts such as discerning of spirits enable effective witnessing. The believer is better equipped to identify hidden evil in those we seek to convert.

IMPARTATION

"Do not neglect the gift that is in you, which was given to you by prophecy with the laying on of the hands of the eldership" (1 Tim. 4:14).

Paul spoke to his spiritual son Timothy, reminding him of the grace received at his ordination when the elders of Iconium and Lystra laid hands on him and prophesied destiny into him. The laying on of hands and prophecy are Holy Spirit-employed means of accrediting His servants as appointed leaders. The apostles fasted and prayed, then laid hands on Barnabas and Saul *"for the work to which I have called them"* (Acts 13:2).

Prophecy functions as an important tool in times of strategic spiritual positioning. Paul was not specifically speaking of the gift of prophecy, but in reference to a culmination of supernatural endowments transferred by faith to Timothy through prophetic utterance at his ordination. In Timothy's case he was commissioned on an apostolic mandate after being mentored by Paul. Paul was challenging Timothy as a fivefold apostolic agent with a prophetic mandate to the Church to confront false teaching in the area. It may be said by implication that Timothy received by grace the same intrinsic ability to manifest the Spirit through the gift of prophecy. The purpose was to build up, edify, and comfort the believers under his ministry.

Prophecy is a channel through which divine purposes and plans of God can be transmitted into the lives of believers. Apart from leadership appointment, prophetic utterance was used to establish Timothy's ministry.

RESTORES DIVINE ORDER

The hidden ability of prophecy to serve as a means of restoring order was revealed in the creation testimony—God's action to bring order to a previously disorderly state, *"Then God said"* (Gen. 1:1-3). God could have resolved to leave the earth without form or shape, but He spoke into the disorder to create order. God systematically created life on the earth in line with the order of Heaven. He created the firmaments, set boundaries between moon and sun, day and night, sea and land by speaking His creative Word.

Our Lord Jesus presents another example of prophecy being used to restore order in the way He came to the earth realm. Jesus is the Word of God who came in flesh form to live out His life in fulfillment of predictions of prophets (see Isa. 9:6-7). Prophet Isaiah predicted, *"For unto us a Child is born, unto us a Son is given"* (Isa. 9:6). Isaiah was prophesying hundreds of years before the birth of Jesus Christ served as a bridge between God and man. He saw Jesus as the hope that would restore the human race in relationship to God. Jesus Christ spoke to confirm Isaiah and other prophets who prophesied to Israel of His birth. Jesus warned, *"Do not think that I came to destroy the Law or the Prophets. I did not come to destroy but to fulfill"* (Matt. 5:17). Another great prophet John the Baptist had the task of preparing the way for the coming of Christ, the Anointed One.[309] Interpreting John's assignment leads me to conclude that John, through his ministry, was restoring divine order for men to be spiritually prepared to encounter the Lord.

Announces Change

Prophecy was used to announce a new order or dispensation. When the cries of the Israelites got to Heaven, God heard and raised a prophet in the name of Moses to announce the change of a season to Pharaoh. God promised to anoint Moses' mouth to fulfill his assignment, *"Now therefore, go, and I will be with your mouth and teach you what you shall say"* (Exod. 4:12). Also, in the time before Samuel was born, the Bible narrates the spiritual state of Israel due to lack of *"widespread revelation"* (1 Sam. 3:1). Samuel was used to bring about change and to release the power. When Israel asked for a king, Saul, who became the first king, was impacted by the spirit of prophecy (1 Sam. 10:10). When Saul lost his kingdom through rebellion, God sent Samuel to anoint David as the new king—a new rule was instituted.

Also, at the close of the Old Testament dispensation change was announced through Malachi's prophecy when he spoke of the Messiah to come and John the Baptist who would prepare the hearts of children and fathers (Mal. 4:6). The prophetic ministries of Anna and Simeon continued to work in partnership with Heaven for the coming Messiah (Luke 2:25-32; 36-38). Prophet Joel spoke of a dispensation that would see spiritual gifts generalized (Joel 2:28), and when that time came, the gift of prophecy was distributed to the Church by the Holy Spirit (1 Cor. 12:10). Peter's sermon just after the outpouring on the day of Pentecost announced a new spiritual order. This trend of the Old Testament prophets can be seen also as a New Testament function of the prophetic gift.

Chapter Fourteen

VALUE OF PROPHECY

Aim: To emphasize the value prophecy brings to the local church congregation and to individual Christian witness.

Value means "worth, importance, appeal" and for emphasis *worth,* for instance, means "merit, appeal, significance, attraction, importance, meaning." This chapter explores some qualities embodied in the meaning of value. The spirit of prophecy is the testimony of Jesus' ministry in our lives. The spirit of prophecy bears witness to Jesus as Lord.[310] Thus every word of prophecy whether at the foundational level of exhortation, edification, and comfort or more advanced level of the function of prophet must bear witness to Jesus as Lord.[311]

BIBLICAL INSIGHT

The nature of prophecy as a forth telling, and foretelling gift is evident when practitioners function in divine ability to unveil hidden mysteries in God's written Word through prophetic preaching and teaching. Until revealed *(rhema)*, the written Word of God *(logos)* holds mysteries of His Kingdom. Apostle Paul taught, *"And so we have the prophetic word confirmed, which you do well to heed as a light that shines in a dark place, until the day dawns and the morning star rises in your hearts"* (2 Pet. 1:19). There are several visible prophetic ministries in our time, such as Chuck Pierce, Rick Joyner, and T.D. Jakes, who have the ability to extract wisdom for present times by interpreting the heart of God through His written Word. This ability in T.D. Jakes, for example, has seen many in the black race liberated from oppressive mind-sets. It must be stated that no word of prophecy holds greater authority or validity than the written Word of God. Prophets of old spoke under the inspiration of God's Spirit: *"The law of the Lord is perfect, converting the soul; the testimony of the Lord is sure, making wise the simple"* (Ps. 19:7).

Prophecy must speak out of God's character and nature—a word of rebuke must be characterized by the love of God.[312] Prophecy must be founded on the Word of God. It is always best to have prophetic words confirmed by other prophets: *"Let two or three prophets speak and let the others judge"* (1 Cor. 14:29).

RESTORATION

Prophecy, in its supernatural ability to predict the mind of God, possesses the same innate quality to bring restoration to listeners. In this regard the gift of prophecy awakens hope where hope has been deferred (Prov. 13:12). I remember praying for a friend's daughter who was living under the fear of cancer. The Lord gave me a prophetic word for her that spoke of His faithfulness in her situation. The fear she felt seemed to be diffused by that Word of the Lord and the hope accompanying God's promise to see her through. The Spirit of God spoke to me revealing the birth of a son who would be called Samuel. Within months of the word, Samuel was on his way, and the lump in her breast disappeared in fulfillment of God's Word.

STRATEGIC PRAYER

"To the intent that now the manifold wisdom of God might be made known by the church to the principalities and powers in the heavenly places" (Ephesians 3:10).

Through prophetic sight, strategic level prayer and intercession initiatives can achieve better results. Divine insight gained into previously concealed issues enables intercessors to pray effectively. Spiritual mapping has played a vital role in the intense prayers that overcome demonic strongholds in whole cities. I remember being impacted by a book on prayer evangelism by Ed Silvoso that I read at a time when the Lord was teaching me to enter into the city I was to serve from in the spirit before a natural entry.

Another profound experience came through a prophetic journey I undertook on the leading of the Lord. I was led to put together a team of trusted fearless prayer warriors, mainly from the Prayer School I facilitated in partnership with another ministry. Our assignment would involve prayer walking a part of our city well known for decadence and sexual immorality. The Lord revealed entry points of several sexual spirits into the city that now dominated the entire area. I saw that territory as it appeared in the spiritual realm in an open vision. I was shown the hierarchy of demonic activities in the area, mainly homosexual. Some of the spirits boldly informed me their presence in that part of the city predated mine—going back to the 1930s. For any person not familiar with strategic level spiritual warfare, the demons speak flippantly like legion. They are often keen to reveal information of their activities with the hope that the words "I bind" or "the blood of Jesus" will never be mentioned. Remember, their father, satan, is the father of lies (see John 8:44).

In one aspect of the vision, I was shown a line in the ground that represented a boundary between the gay community and the Chinese community. To my amazement we identified the same boundary on inspection of the grounds in the natural. The strongman over the Chinese quarters told me his section was different from the homosexual quarters and that the gay community was not allowed into their section. I stood on the boundary line in the natural amazed, especially after having shared details of the quite lengthy open vision with the team before embarking on our assignment.

Other spiritual demarcations revealed the extent of demonic activities in the city and the existence of many territories, each guarded by a strongman (see Matt. 12:29). One particular bar with a blasphemous name and menu named after parts of the human anatomy had us gutted. We were led to pray outside the bar with its Egyptian-style décor exhibiting unbelievable profanities. Our hearts appeared to have been touched corporately by the love of Jesus Christ as we wept in prayer, calling for deliverance of men and women bound by homosexuality. No person is born an accident and not one person created by God deserves to suffer from identity crisis. The demons that create confusion in minds of men and women were the ones I was shown arguing over boundaries.

We were led of the Spirit of God to call for the God of Elijah who helped him battle the 400 prophets of Baal. We suddenly understood the plight of the Church, especially as so many believers would never imagine or believe the experience I now narrate. We cried for God's mercy over our city (see Ezek. 22:30). As we stood outside the bar early on the morning of June 1, 2003, the area gradually started coming alive. The street we were on was to be the center for the annual gay pride community festival.

Eleven days after our prayer for mercy for the city, for deliverance of our brothers and sisters bound to the gay spirit, and for the provocative club, a local radio station reported a fire in that particular bar, but fortunately no one was hurt. God's love and mercy for all creation was evident in that no one met with harm in the fire. The bar was boarded up for a considerable length of time confirming what the Lord spoke to my heart—that it would take a "sustained attack" to uproot the evil that sought to take over the area. Insight received from the Holy Spirit about that prayer assignment enabled me and the team to pray strategically. We connected with God as the sign of fire called for manifesting in the natural. To sustain victory in spiritual warfare in a case such as described, a Word of the Lord would need to be heard. The role of prophecy in spiritual warfare cannot be underestimated, especially when the aim is to unseat demonic rule in an area. Wisdom dictates that we partner with Heaven for meaningful spiritual victory: *"The testimony of the Lord is sure, making wise the simple"* (Ps. 19:7).

DANIEL—YESTERDAY AND TODAY

When Daniel understood the time for the end of Israel's captivity he prayed, *"Then I set my face toward the Lord God to make request by prayer and supplications, with fasting, sackcloth and ashes"* (Dan. 9:3). Daniel's understanding did not emerge through a natural state, but as a result of God's prophetic grace on his life. Daniel's case emphasizes the importance of prophecy endowment in shifting times and seasons over a nation. The 2005 Berlin Reconciliation effort I mentioned earlier is one such initiative that appears to have read God's prophetic clock accurately. I believe Africa is the next continent to experience economic revival and restoration, while the future of Europe hangs in the balance with much-needed prayer lacking. I believe that it makes natural and spiritual sense for those whose ancestors literally raped the soil of Africa of every bit of dignity to stand in humility and to appease the living God. Assisting in this African rebirth would be an amazing act of honor, one I believe would serve as powerful currency for intercessors seeking to shift spiritual darkness pushing to cover Europe.

Daniel represents the prophetic in an Old Testament time relevant and applicable to our time. As a matter of fact, Daniel's role in praying for the deliverance of Israel lends support to the message of this book—to see the entire Body of Christ activated in spiritual gifts for the sake of the lost. A Jew by birth, Daniel was trained in the non-Christian environment of Babylon along with other Jews in exile. Daniel had to learn the culture of the Chaldeans, his captors (see Dan. 1:4-5). He learned the art of spiritual warfare amid the sorcerers, diviners, and witches who regularly consulted with the king (see Dan. 2:2). His faith in God was tested through King Nebuchadnezzar's fiery furnace and lion's den, but through these trials Daniel remained in partnership with Heaven. Applying principles revealed through Daniel's life to the average Christian experience leaves a lot to be desired. Daniel was a man of prevailing prayers, and his strong prayer ministry sustained his tenacious life.

Spiritual Warfare

With benefit of insight into lives, circumstances, and situations, a prayer warrior is better prepared to resist forces of darkness that wage war against fulfillment of prophecies as in the case of Daniel. The Prince of the Kingdom of Persia waged war against angel Gabriel dispatched with answers to Daniel's prayers for his nation. This demonic principality withstood the angel for 21 days.[313] The Prince of Persia recognized the time for change. He knew the hour for Israel's deliverance from captivity had come. He sought to hinder answers to Daniel's prayer for revelation.

There are times when the Lord reveals the spiritual atmosphere around me with a command to declare. Often at these times he reveals activities of "familiar spirits" that I have now come to identify as common with areas where Islamic activities are predominant. These spirits become desperate to negate activities of the Church, but since the devil does not have access to third heaven communication, the devil wages intense war in the second and first heavens against believers. Intense activities of diviners create "pathways" in the spiritual realm for cloning spirits to mirror image genuine prophetic activities. Prophets in our time must partner with the Lord, especially in the realms of strategic level spiritual warfare. Daniel's prayer was also timely because he had understanding of the seasons and times of God for Israel (see 1 Chron. 12:32).

Angelic Assistance

The Bible records Daniel's experience and partnership with angel Gabriel: "*Whom I had seen in the vision at the beginning*" (Dan. 9:21). The prophetic realm invites partnership with angels: "*Gabriel, make this man understand the vision*" (Dan. 8:16). On one occasion the angel informed him: "*O Daniel, I have now come forth to give you skill to understand*" (Dan. 9:22). Archangel Gabriel also appeared to Daniel with interesting news of activity in the spiritual realm, Daniel said, "*He informed me, and talked with me, and said, 'O, Daniel, I have now come forth to give you skill to understand'*" (Dan. 10:22).

Daniel received revelation of the times but lacked necessary skills to unravel the mystery of Israel's deliverance. Another example is seen with Peter, who needed to come into revelation of times and to then understand the time had come for the salvation of all, not just the Jews (see Acts 10:3-4; 12:7)

RENEWED HOPE

Knowing the heart of God offers renewed hope, especially in cases when ongoing problems exist. It is a known fact that hearts of men grow weary when prolonged time of prayer fails to yield desired results. Prophecy inspires such hearts and reignites passion to serve the Lord. They are subsequently able to function out of renewed hope instead of apathy and complacency. Knowing the mind of Christ provides a believer with assurance of purpose and strength to achieve. Every believer is born with a unique destiny worth pursuing. The influence of direct prophetic utterances that confirm the divine will of God for a person's life is ever so comforting. Paul charged his spiritual son Timothy not to neglect his gifts (see 1 Tim. 4:14). A person receiving prophetic words must believe in the ability of God's Word to recreate their circumstances. Prophecies should be watered with faith and prayer. First Timothy 4:14 also reveals the significant value of prophecy during ordination of ministers as a means of imparting spiritual gifts. Also, apostle Paul admonished Timothy who was commissioned and sent to challenge the teaching of false doctrine in the church in Ephesus at that time.[314]

EVANGELISM

The gift of prophecy transforms lives when exercised correctly and with maturity. I have had several personal experiences when people's lives were transformed through prophetic words given. I remember experiencing a low point in my ministry life during 2001. I longed to understand the Lord's purpose for my life, especially as I had experienced difficulty settling down in England despite spending more years of my life in England than the nation of my birth (Nigeria).

The restlessness I felt in my spirit came to an end during a prayer summit in London held in the same year. One evening I was asked to take up an offering. The guest speaker was to be Cindy Jacobs of Generals of Intercession, U.S.A. Cindy walked onto the platform while I was still there, and proceeded to prophesy over my life with incredible accuracy that revealed my destiny in England. She declared, "England is your destiny," and finished by praying, "the anointing you have given me on my life, give it to her Lord, give it to her." Shortly after this incident my life and prophetic ministry were transformed. I felt happier and more confident knowing I was in the right place at the right time (England). My husband and I lived for the time we could move over to the United States, but God had called us to England with a timetable that would effectively have us resident in Britain until a given date, and thereafter to function out of another spiritual base.

After that experience the Lord started giving me deeper insight into the nation's redemptive gifts. I received greater understanding of spiritual climates over Britain and more particularly of England. Prophecy in this case helped me re-engage with my calling to England and to settle down to task. My prayer life was also transformed as I seemed to embrace destiny more comfortably. The burden I had for the nations of Britain and of England increased.

REVEALS DEEP SECRETS

Prophecy reveals deep secrets, even secrets of the heart. At the foundational level of inspirational prophecy, deep secrets of another's life may not be revealed. Paul encourages us to prophesy according to the measure of the prophesier's faith, *"Having then gifts differing according to the grace that is given to us, if prophecy, let us prophesy according to the proportion of faith."*[315] I remembered giving a word of prophecy for a president of an African nation. The contents of the prophecy were only previously known to the president—and to God. The impact of this accurate prophecy led the president into a lengthy fast. When the heart of a president is turned to God, the nation turns also.

Chapter Fifteen

—◦ ▣◆▣ ◦—

EXERCISING THE GIFT
OF PROPHECY

Aim: Exposition of apostle Paul's teachings to the church in
   Corinth on spiritual gifts, with focus on the gift of
   prophecy. Ultimately, this chapter seeks to extract principles for gift application in the New Testament church
   for the benefit of the Church body today.

*For you can all prophesy one by one, that **all may learn and
all be encouraged***[316] (1 Corinthians 14:31).

According to the teaching of apostle Paul in First Corinthians
14:31, all believers in Christ Jesus can prophesy, and should earnestly
pursue exercising prophecy as a matter of course.

The reason is twofold: to create awareness and learning in the gift
of prophecy.

We read about Saul and the sons of the prophets in First Samuel
10. The sons of the prophets were exercising prophecy as a matter of
calling, as a matter of course in line with the mantle of prophet over
their lives. Saul was instructed: *"Then the Spirit of the Lord will come*

upon you, and you will prophesy with them, and be turned into another man" (1 Sam. 10:6). Saul received impartation of the grace of prophecy that was on the company of prophets individually and corporately. By way of confirmation of the gift imparted in Saul, he began to prophesy as the sons of the prophets did. The account of Saul and the sons of the prophets should read as an inspiration to those who desire to exercise their gift of prophecy. God has never changed, a fact easily seen in the transformation experienced by Saul who prophesied and became a new man.

Through mature administration and practice of prophecy, others learn and the entire Body of Christ is encouraged. In the case of Saul, he did not go on to serve as prophet to Israel—he became king. The purpose of God was fulfilled in Saul prophesying when he did. The future king of Israel was being turned into a new man by the power of God through prophecy. Saul's experience in prophesying while not a prophet can be interpreted for present-day understanding as a confirmation of prophet Joel's words (Joel 2:28).

Similarly the purpose of God will be fulfilled should believers start to exercise prophecy and other gifts of the Holy Spirit regularly, as a matter of mission. There were no formal instructions in application of the gift in the case of Saul; however, as the sons of the prophets were in the course of prophesying, Saul received the supernatural gift of prophecy by indirect impartation. The prophetic gift lies within born-again, Holy Spirit-filled believers by virtue of our new identity in Christ's resurrection.

Another reference to prophecy I have personally been impacted by is from apostle Paul's admonition to his spiritual son Timothy to *"stir up the gift of God which is in you through the laying on of my hands"* (2 Tim. 1:6). In line with Paul's word to Timothy, believers seeking to exercise their gift may be activated by a fivefold servant prophet by virtue of their calling to equip saints for the work of the ministry. Teaching also exposes us to the Holy Spirit's activation—for the testimony of Jesus is the spirit of prophecy (see Rev. 19:10).

All May Be Encouraged

Prophecy is the ability to speak the mind and heart of God. It has been described as "the express thoughts of God spoken in a language that no man in his natural gift of speech could articulate on his own."[317] It would be accurate to conclude then that those who speak God's heart must speak with accuracy and confidence (see Amos 3:8). Prophecy is the outflow of God's heart not limited to time, but in time is fulfilled (see Eccles. 3:11). With the benefit of the Issachar anointing the Church will receive present-day understanding of God's heart. God speaks out of His nature. His Word spoken out of the mouths of His followers ought to reflect His nature (Jer. 9:23-24). God is love[318] and even when He chastens, He chastens with love. Thus, any person claiming to speak God's Word must speak as a representative of God's heart. His heart is the storehouse of His blessing, holding His will for His children.

Chapter Sixteen

⊷⊷ ⊱◈⊰ ⊶⊶

PROPHETIC EXPECTATIONS

Aim: To highlight areas of advantage for the interest of local church leadership.

IN THE NEW TESTAMENT CHURCH & TODAY

The Book of Acts account of the outpouring of the Holy Spirit, which occurred when Pentecost had fully come (in Christ Jesus), records Peter's speech which referenced the prophecy of prophet Joel. In that instance, Peter used Joel's prophecy to explain the manifestations of the supernatural to the amazement of all present at the time. Although the gift of tongues was the prevalent gift in operation on that occasion, Peter recites portions of Joel chapter 2, when prophecy is mentioned as a sign of the age to come.[319] The outpouring of the Holy Spirit under the new covenant, unlike in the old, was upon *"all flesh."* This phenomenon opened a new dispensation foreshadowed by Joel's prophecy.

The call in our time through the Issachar Mandate and prophetic engagement is for the prophetic church to again interpret the times in

171

context of the mission at hand. The Church's expression of the heart of God must be seen as the spiritual magnet the world is waiting for.[320] I often encourage myself with Paul's declaration to the Corinthians to the point where I recite his words as a preamble to many messages I have preached just so I set personal targets. Paul boldly stated:

> *And my speech and my preaching were not with persuasive words of human wisdom, but in demonstration of the Spirit and of power, that your faith should not be in the wisdom of men but in the power of God (1 Corinthians 2:4-5).*

The practice of spiritual gifts including prophecy is one purpose of the Holy Spirit fullness. The Church cannot therefore shortchange herself by abandoning supernatural abilities given for enhanced worship and effective ministry. Paul was in effect saying that his words were accredited by the Holy Spirit's power to transform.

RELEASING THE GIFT IN SAINTS

In First Corinthians 14:31, Paul the apostle taught, *"For you can all prophesy one by one, that all may learn and all may be comforted."*

In this chapter, I address areas of concern in church or congregational acceptance of spiritual gifts. It is important to note that though the Greek word charisma (which defines "gift") suggests that charismatic believers function in one or more spiritual gifts—that is not necessarily true in practice. Charismatic churches do not routinely welcome public practice of the spiritual gifts written about in First Corinthians 12, Romans 12, and Ephesians 4. We must not give up trying to convince the Church of the qualities these gifts bring to the gathered Church and ultimately to the unsaved whose conversion we are corporately responsible for.

Gift of prophecy in operation would add value and vitality to congregational worship. The Bible appears to suggest listeners become more enlightened and comforted by clarity that proceeds from knowing the mind of Christ. The teachings of apostle Paul regarding prophetic ministry in a church must now be seriously considered, particularly in these last days as evil increases in our world. The Bible warns us that people will develop itchy ears, and false doctrines will dominate the minds of many in the last days:

> For the time will come when they will not endure sound doctrine, but according to their own desires, because they have itching ears, they will heap up for themselves teachers; and they will turn their ears away from truth, and be turned aside to fables (2 Timothy 4:3-4).

The importance of training in correct exercise of spiritual gifts cannot be overemphasized for a people called to outdoor activities in present-day cosmopolitan societies. Several nations are considering laws with the possible effect of clamping down on evangelism. This is even more reason we must embrace the Issachar Mandate and formulate Holy Spirit-inspired strategies to further our assignments. So much emphasis has been placed on prophecy in the Body of Christ in the last decade, but not enough time has been given to training the saints in effective use of the gift. The Church's immediate dilemma revolves around progression of existing prophetic movements, emerging prophetic streams, and the fact that a major part of the Church remains ignorant about spiritual gifts. Some Christians do not believe spiritual gifts are relevant in our time.

Fulfilling the great commission of our Lord Jesus must become the primary pursuit of the Church, and not simply seeking the power of God. Once we have the right order then sorting out divine enablement would not be such a laborious task. The ministries of great men and women of God such as Pastor Benny Hinn, Kenneth Hagin, and Mahesh and Bonnie Chavda are living testimonies of the importance of spiritual gifts such as healing diseases. When the Church embraces her primary responsibility to reach the world with the light of the Gospel, Heaven will back up our actions with power (Mark 16:20).

Church Prophetic

Paul taught, "Let all things be done decently and in order." (1 Cor. 14:40).

The time has come for the Church to embark on house sorting and cleaning. Since the identities of the fivefold function in men need to be uncovered, we are probably expecting too much by simply declaring time to train the saints. Several biblicists and theologians have written excellently about ministries of the fivefold. I suppose with pastors, evangelists, and teachers we do not need much revelation to understand their function. These offices have been functioning actively with the Church. But with apostles, for instance, fresh revelation and interpretative tools are needed to give words to the new apostolic shape. The Church as a body needs to understand that apostles are no longer necessarily male church planters. Our minds need to be prepared to receive the Bob Geldorfs and Bonos of our time, pop stars who are used of God to bring the plight of the poor to platforms around the globe.

Spiritual gifts need to be fully exercised in our church services, prayer meetings, and street evangelism programs. Church leaderships need to consider the idea of appointing a resident or in-house prophet. Such a person assumes the responsibility of introducing training of others in the church to use the gift accurately so that order is maintained in the services. My friend Dr. Paula Price has written extensively on this subject.

Church evangelism strategies will experience boosts if aided by supernatural knowledge and insight into the sufferings of those we are to impact. I remember ministering to an aide to a president of an African nation. His wife was so keen for his salvation that she gave me all sorts of tips on what to do, but I assured her we would be better off praying for manifestations of God's supernatural power. Miracles speak for themselves and for God. The Lord gave me such accurate prophetic words for the Presidential aide that he has now become a committed Christian, and remains in a strategic government position. This principle is recorded in the sayings of Solomon the wise: *"A man's gift makes room for him, and brings him before great men"* (Prov. 18:16).

The narrative of Jesus and the Samaritan woman at Jacob's well confirms the impact of prophecy on evangelism. On that occasion alone, the Bible records many in Samaria believed Jesus was the Lord, the Savior: *"And many of the Samaritans of that city believed in Him because of the word of the woman who testified, 'He told me all that I ever did'"* (John 4:39). At present the world of the occult and new age mysticism appear to be in direct competition with the Church for the hearts and minds of people. The prince of the power of the air is recognized as the *"spirit who now works in the sons of disobedience"* (Eph. 2:2). Spiritual battles will need to be fought if the Church is to disengage the enemy who unfortunately has locked himself through demonic operations into the lives of men and women. The devil administers his evil schemes through a hierarchy of wickedness.[321]

Spiritual gifts must be encouraged as a matter of course if believers are to dislodge and dismantle demonic establishments in their communities. Jesus taught that unless the strongman captivating the hearts of the lost is bound, our efforts will not yield much fruit.[322] The gift of discernment enables believers to determine demonic activities of the strongman in their cities.

We Grow When We Hear

In line with the teachings of Paul, the Church will blossom into a healthy body enjoying numerical growth, with members enlightened and comforted by the voice of God.

I remember times during Sunday services in the church I attended before I assumed the duties of a pastor myself. Whenever the spirit of prophecy was present in a service, it was almost invariable for a prophecy or message in tongues to come forth through one of the leaders or a trusted member. Often when an interpretation to the message was spoken through a recognized leader, it would be met with joy and clapping from the congregation. I remember such Sundays and they hold a special place in my heart. I often left the service feeling connected with the Father in Heaven on those occasions.

I recollect my first reaction when, as a young prophetic minister, I realized I understood and could interpret divine tongues when spoken by others. Too embarrassed to tell anyone, I resolved to keep my secret to myself. On more than one occasion I knew and recognized error in interpretation of a message given, but it did not seem to matter because I was only too glad to hear from Heaven in church. But if I was honest, I believe those instances affected me adversely and left me slightly unsure of the exercise of the gift of interpretation of tongues. My experiences with hearing wrong, or at times incomplete, interpretations put me off exercising that spiritual gift myself.

PASTORS ARE KEY

Pastors are key to achieving the Issachar Mandate and to encouraging prophetic engagement. Pastors play a crucial role in the call for repositioning of the prophetic gift from within church buildings to out into our communities. Pastors have been known to reject prophecy for good and not so good reasons. I do believe some cases of immaturity have led to the pulpit insecurity that exists. The Lord will not give a prophet a message for a pastor that redirects the focus of the church unless such a pastor allows it. God is a God of order. Prophets will usually be used to bring pastors of churches confirmation of insight rather than introduce new direction to the church.

All believers occupy special, unique places in the heart of Father. As a matter of fact if divine responsibilities are placed in the right order, prophets and other fivefold function are servant leaders. Pastors are to make their flock available to receive specialist training. Training such as in the use of the gift of prophecy will enhance their ability to fulfill their own destiny. Pastors need to discern, or check through natural means, the integrity of a mantle or prophetic ministry. It is not for a pastor to hold back another person's destiny. In my experience, both as a prophetic saint called to serve in various office functions and now serving as a pastor, I can say that the heart of Christ is for pastors to release the potential of God in the people they serve as leader. The hearts of true fivefold pastors are in sync with the Lord's desire. The quality that exemplified my one time pastor was his willingness to explore releasing the purpose of God in my life.

WISDOM IS ANOTHER KEY

The Bible urges: *"Wisdom is the principle thing; therefore get wisdom. And in all your getting, get understanding"* (Prov. 4:7).

A prophetic person is required to operate in divine wisdom, not caution. Solomon the wise, speaking of wisdom's house, points to wisdom's columns as complete; her pillars are numbered seven (Prov. 9:1). As mentioned previously, seven is God's number for completion and perfection. Although the value of prophecy in context of church worship is adequately covered in the Bible, the fact is slightly different in practice. I sincerely believe the problem of immature prophetic ministries has been worsened by greedy prophets whose sole motivation is to get out their latest revelation. Training programs need to feature more on protocol and etiquette of this high calling. Jesus Christ's ministry should be our model and referral point for present-day prophetic ministry. Immature prophetic believers ought not to be condoned or pampered by prophets. Truth should be at the foundation of every leadership training program.

A pastor may be in a prophet's life for a season to be used to prepare a prophet for the future. Imagine the fate of Joseph's family if he never spent time in the pit. I am personally grateful to my no-nonsense, former pastor, pastor David Carr. For 11 years I went through the process of maturity under his watchful eyes. My journey included betrayal by fellow Hebrews,[323] to exile in Midian,[324] to hearing the voice of God in the burning bush[325]. I overcame fears to stand before Pharaoh as the servant of "I Am Who I Am."[326] Like Jacob I humbly learned to serve for Rebecca and to be given Leah[327] instead, but knew when to wave goodbye to Uncle Laban,[328] to reject Saul's armor,[329] and to trust my sling and five stones[330]. There is no promotion for a prophetic person who does not learn to reject the king's wine and delicacies,[331] to trust God in the fiery furnace[332]. A prophet must learn to trust the Lord to shut the mouth of lions,[333] to confront Baal's prophets,[334] and to ignore Sanballats and Tobiahs[335]. The Bible encourages believers: *"He who calls you is faithful, who also will do it"* (1 Thess. 5:24).

There was never a need to strive or draw attention to oneself, so I developed a practice of writing down prophetic words then forwarding the same to my pastor, his assistant, or any other leader present at the service. My credibility was never questioned, so the need to justify myself as prophetic did not arise. The Lord creates opportunities for gift application if the prophetic are able to endure the process that makes a prophet a prophet of distinction. A prophet is first and foremost a servant. Whenever I received an important prophetic word for the pastor outside of service time, I telephoned the pastor's secretary to alert her. Pressuring a leader for the sake of a prophetic word shows a level of immaturity in the prophetic saint requiring attention.

Once my piece of paper containing prophetic insight was delivered to my pastor during a service, I felt relieved and never watched his reaction. It did not seem to matter whether my word from the Lord was read out or not; I had implicit trust in the pastor's decision. Through this practice, the Spirit of the Lord was training my spirit to be content, trusting God's ability to establish me.

It is important for pastors and churches to emulate the practice of my pastor, who like many pastors was not particularly enamored by prophets and those claiming to be prophetic. However, he was genuinely willing to assist capable prophetic ministries, unlike some other pastors who blatantly frustrated the gift in their members due to previous bad experiences. I must respectfully submit my opinion that it is dangerous for the destinies of God's children to be controlled by bad experiences of one person who happens to be the pastor. As a matter of fact, my pastor and his assistant entrusted me with what I considered then to be a huge responsibility: to create awareness of prophecy and the prophetic through a series in our church's magazine. The first time prophecy was ever given such profile in our church was through those magazine articles. That initial opportunity provided the foundation now, as this book is a progression and an example of the advantage in encouraging believers to develop their spiritual gift.

IN-HOUSE TRAINING PROGRAMS HELP

Another important factor to deliberate on and to take cognizance in seeking development of the prophetic gift in churches would be church programming. I would have benefited tremendously from an in-house structured program for training in prophetic ministry. Such a program needs to give considerable attention to the protocol of prophetic ministry to deal with the pitfalls many pastors dread. My church went one step ahead of others to see that spiritual gifts were not stifled. Although the predominant gift in operation in our church was the gift of tongues, I doubt many of us could differentiate between the experience of interpreted tongues and that of prophecy. I am of the opinion that more of the Holy Spirit's gifts would have been manifested if the congregation understood, through teaching, our divine right to operate in supernatural endowments.

CHURCH PROPHET

...having been built on the foundation of the apostles and prophets, Jesus Christ Himself being the chief cornerstone (Ephesians 2:20).

The church prophet should be a person within the church leadership with a credible, recognized prophetic mantle. A prophet, like any other believer, enjoys the same Holy Spirit- enabled ability to manifest prophecy. However, a prophet has the added responsibility of his or her gift serving as a gift to the Body of Christ. A primary aspect of the mandate of a prophet in leadership in a local church would be to recognize prophetic members. Such members are then placed in a mentoring program led by the church prophet as a part of the church's training program. The church may also invite expertise of recognized independent ministries who should be affiliated with a local church with tested training programs. It is extremely important that any person claiming to function in the mantle of prophet is able to submit their ministry to a network of accountability: *"The spirits of the prophets are subject to the prophets"* (1 Cor. 14:32). The local

179

church training program can then link with other regional or national initiatives.

HUMILITY IS ANOTHER KEY

Humility is a key ingredient for any successful prophetic ministry to be achieved. In seeking to redress the effects of past hurts, malpractices, and other errors on church leadership, believers seeking to operate spiritual gifts must learn the secret power of humility. While it can be said that the position of some in leadership in rejecting spiritual gifts is not an option, the onus is on those professing to operate in these gifts to paint a different picture. The Church needs to understand the times to know the strategy of Heaven for vision fulfillment. But to win divine favor we must be in God's divine will. I do believe the Church, at least in Britain, needs to humbly admit that we desperately need the Lord's power and abilities to survive the pressures—from Islam, for instance.

To encourage God's heart to see the saints mobilized and trained, a general procedure for practice of prophecy in congregational services should be drawn up and publicized in church bulletins. The Church is still the initial training ground for the works of Jesus. Jesus declared His public ministry in a synagogue, but then spent the rest of His life outside the synagogue fulfilling His mandate (Luke 4:18). The nature of prophetic ministry requires due attention to be given to procedural matters to assure order in services.

Prophecy enjoys tremendous profile in the eyes of the average believer, so any malpractices can have adverse effects on an entire church body. Since the Bible makes clear the position of prophets in God's agenda, both in the Old and New Testament, the Church cannot afford to brush aside this divine gift or those endowed to serve in the capacity of prophetic trainers. The simple, logical solution would be for the pastor to release a church prophet who is a part of his or her leadership team. It then falls on the shoulders of such a person to prepare the church in her function as the prophetic bride through teaching programs. Through this practice the purpose of spiritual gifts outlined in First Corinthians 12, Romans 12, and Ephesians 4 will be fulfilled.

THE LORD IS WAITING

Behold I stand at the door and knock. If anyone hears My voice and opens the door, I will come in to him and dine with him, and he with Me (Revelation 3:20).

In my case, I was particularly conscious of not being seen as the resident church prophet in my local church—despite enjoying the pastor's approval and blessing to practice prophecy. If that were the case, I would have taken up some other person's spiritual position and attracted out-of-time wars. Prophetic ministries must seek understanding of spiritual boundaries. I had come to understand after working with a dynamic prophet named Dr. Paula Price of Everlasting Ministries, USA, the necessity of identifying a resident church prophet. The idea of a church prophet may not appeal to every church. There are some pastors who will never embrace prophetic ministry nor establish an office responsibility of prophet. Again, we must all be able to function in liberty of revelation. I do not believe in prophetic ministries bulldozing their way into churches—neither do I believe in false submission to ungodly leadership. God will work all things for the good of those who trust in Him; hence, we must make the pursuit of God our primary calling.

A church prophet serves as God's messenger and representative on the leadership of a local church. Prophets are not being singled out as the only representatives of God in the church, but I must be faithful to the message I am seeking to disseminate. Such a person assists members with dream interpretations, discerning of spirits, prophetic prayer strategies, and prophetic evangelism programs. After all, the work of the fivefold is to equip the saints in all awareness of spiritual matters. An informed believer is the devil's worst nightmare. An equipped believer is more able to handle natural challenges while conducting spiritual business.

Church Prophets Interpret Spiritual Matters

In my case, having realized the position of church prophet was not for me; my energies were then channeled toward championing the cause of releasing the prophetic gift and the prophets. A church prophet, being an active member of the church leadership team, is the appropriate person to offer prayer or any other support on the pastor's agreement. In cases of ambiguity that sometime arise with prophecies spoken in public, a church prophet would be expected to bring clarity. The truth is unless the Church fills spiritual positions ordained in the Bible, the necessary power will elude us. A church prophet is the person given responsibility for words of certain spiritual weight to match spiritual responsibilities, including that of a translator. It is the prophet who has to interpret a prophetic message to the congregation to encourage personal application. Agabus's prophecy of worldwide famine led to matching action to prevent unnecessary harm (see Acts 11:28). The mandate of Issachar demands the present-day Church assume the role of the Church in the early age. Aside from prophesying, interpretation of the revelation led to a practical solution affecting Christians and non-Christians alike. The expectation of a member who does not clearly serve in a fivefold function is to exercise the gift of prophecy for exhortation, edification, and comfort. Not every believer is called to the more advanced Agabus-type function. I strongly believe that no person can be endowed with any spiritual ability beyond their level of spiritual maturity and disposition: *"As God has dealt to each one a measure of faith"* (Rom. 12:3). The weight of prophetic words entrusted to a prophet differs from that given to a saint not functioning in the gifts.

Chapter Seventeen

PROPHECY AND TONGUES

Aim: To bring clarity and interpretation of the gift of prophecy and tongues, especially when exercised in congregational worship.

The value uplifting words from the Lord brings to lives, especially when spoken in time, remains unquantifiable. Apostle Paul said, *"I wish you all spoke with tongues, but even more that you prophesied"* (1 Cor. 14:5).

I have included this chapter in an attempt to address an area of common confusion. I was once asked if the messages in tongues classified as prophecies. Paul's endorsement of the gift of prophecy over the gift of tongues in a corporate setting must be understood in context of his expressed desire to see Christians at the time become all God desired them to be.

To the church of God which is at Corinth, to those who are sanctified in Christ Jesus, called to be saints, with all who in every place call on the name of the Jesus Christ our Lord, both theirs and ours....I thank my God always concerning you for the grace of God which was given to you by Christ Jesus, that you were enriched in every thing by Him in all utterance and all knowledge, even as the testimony of Christ was confirmed in you, so that you come short in no gift, eagerly waiting for the revelation of our Lord Jesus Christ (1 Corinthians 1:2,4-7).

DEALING WITH FOUNDATIONAL ISSUES CHURCHES FACE

Apostle Paul established the church in Corinth about A.D. 50-51 during an 18-month period on his second missionary journey. First Corinthians is basically a pastoral letter written by Paul in response to news of idolatry, divisive philosophies, and other malpractices in the church. Paul was therefore dealing with doctrinal and practical issues as opposed to laying an ambush on the gift of tongues. Corinth was one of the most important commercial cities at the time. The city was infamous for paganism, idolatry, and all manner of permissiveness. Aphrodite (Venus), the goddess of licentious love, was known to be the chief deity of the city. Part of her worship involved a thousand prostitutes licensed to serve at the temple dedicated to her. It was no wonder then that the prevalent spirit would transfer into the church. The Lord Jesus taught about the importance of binding the strongman before effective evangelism can be achieved. Jesus said, *"Or how can one enter a strong man's house and plunder his goods, unless he first binds the strong man? And then he will plunder his house"* (Matt. 12:29).

Foundational issues had to be resolved as a way of safeguarding the work of the Lord that had been planted among the Greeks. Again the Lord emphasized the need to destroy strongholds by destroying the force that established such strongholds in the first place. He said, *"But when a stronger than he comes upon him and overcomes him, he takes from him all his armor in which he trusted, and divides his spoils"* (Luke 11:22).

Paul cannot be said to have personally preferred prophecy over tongues or be said to have encouraged believers to prefer prophecy over tongues. He had previously expressed his heart as a father in the faith to see all believers, even beyond Corinth *"come short in no gift."* He wanted everyone under his mentorship armed with supernatural abilities to deal with spiritual challenges. Paul was addressing a pattern and order for service with a view to establishing a workable structure in the church. Spiritual gifts needed to be in their preferred perspective to achieve divine purpose. It was important for Christians to walk worthy of their calling—as it is today.

Reading Paul's words from First Corinthians 1 "...even as the testimony of Christ was confirmed in you" in conjunction with Revelation 19:10: *"For the testimony of Jesus is the spirit of prophecy,"* amplifies the message I have tried to reinforce, that every believer in Jesus must desire spiritual gifts, especially prophecy as evidence of Jesus alive in us. The Church bears the testimony of Jesus; the challenge is to get out onto the streets and "tell it."

PERSONAL EDIFICATION VERSUS CORPORATE BLESSING

He who speaks in tongues edifies himself, but he who prophecies edifies the church (1 Corinthians 14:4).

Speaking in tongues is for personal edification and personal devotion: *"For he who speaks in a tongue does not speak to men but to God"* (1 Cor. 14:2). Prophecy, while having a place for personal edification, is primarily for corporate edification. When the speaking of tongues is accompanied by interpretation, the Church is edified because worshipers understand the message. In the experiences drawn from my church, it was evident that the gift of speaking in tongues was the dominant gift in operation, although I am not entirely sure of the reason. However, the divine messages were often interpreted by a recognized leader. Can you imagine the effect on worshipers of a message in tongues with no interpretation?

DON'T WORSHIP GIFTS

Since Paul was addressing doctrinal issues, his focus was rightfully on achieving practical, workable objectives. The Greeks had a tendency to default into idolatry, so Paul challenged their innate attitudes:

But now, brethren, if I come to you speaking with tongues, what shall I profit you unless I speak to you either by revelation, by knowledge, by prophesying, or by teaching? (1 Corinthians 14:6).

Paul spoke in tongues himself: *"I thank my God I speak with tongues more than you all"* (1 Cor. 14:18). But his concern was for order to be maintained in congregational worship so that unbelievers who attended were edified. As a prophetic community with a mandate to reach the world regardless of culture, the Body of Christ needs to teach about aspects of spiritual gifts to avoid the same pitfalls Paul was addressing. The tendency of the Greeks was to worship knowledge, a trend that is identifiable in the Western church today. Some have termed this unfortunate disposition "the Greek mind-set." It would not have been surprising for the believers in Corinth to relapse into idolizing tongues, so Paul carefully expounded on biblical truth. As Paul recognized, *"Greeks seek after wisdom"* (1 Cor. 1:22).

TIME TO GROW UP!

When I was a child, I spoke as a child, I understood as a child, I thought as a child; but when I became a man, I put away childish things (1 Corinthians 13:11).

The Holy Spirit works with the Church to edify; so any evidence of His presence in a service confirms that all things work in order. We need "hearts shift" as messengers of Christ to embrace the social needs around us. If the gift of prophecy is exercised correctly, congregations will experience greater levels of spiritual maturity, taking their witness outside of church buildings to the hurting. I am reminded of the developmental process babies go through at different stages from sitting up to crawling to standing and then taking a few steps. Every step of a baby's development marks a step toward independence. A baby's first steps are often celebrated by joyful parents. Then the child bides time until confident enough to stroll into active life.

I liken the case of the baby to the Church. Believers must be encouraged into maturity by the fivefold leaders. It is the sole responsibility of the Church to win back the souls of the lost who strengthen the hands of the occult through incessant searching for ways of filling voids in their personal lives. We have seen an increase in new age religions and psychic fairs, while humanism and secularism compete with the laws of God.

The passion of my heart to see the Church rise to the full stature of the image of Christ can only be captured by apostle Paul's words: *"Now concerning spiritual gifts, brethren, I do not want you to be ignorant"* (1 Cor. 12:1). Paul expressed his passion for the Church to understand the history, theology, and practice of spiritual gifts. Whether practiced in or out of church, spiritual gifts are given not for personal promotion, but are for Kingdom expansion (Matt. 24:14). Peter encouraged men to speak as *"oracles of God"* (1 Pet. 4:11).

ENDNOTES

1. Luke 17:20.

2. Luke 17:21.

3. Acts 15:1.

4. Amos 9:11-12.

5. Acts 15:7.

6. Acts 15:28.

7. Acts 15:26.

8. Matt. 24:6-14.

9. Matt. 24:5; 2 Tim. 4:3-4.

10. Matt. 24:11.

11. Eccles. 3:1,11,17.

12. Luke 2:25-35.

13. Luke 2:36-38.

14. Anna was a prophetess who spent her time in the temple.

15. Jeremiah spoke of the number of years Israel would be enslaved before their redemption.

16. Jeremiah 29:10.

17. John 14:6.

18. Luke 1:77.

19. Verse 10.

20. Edited and published by Rev. Patrick Stevenson in December 2002. Available from Arise Missions Publications: www.womenarisepray.org.

21. *Word For Israel & The Church* recorded on prophecy page: www.womenarisepray.org.

22. Rev. 22:12-20.

23. Acts 2:14-39; Acts 17:19-23; Acts 8:18-24–13:6-1.

24. Matt. 5:17.

25. Matt. 24:6-7.

26. Matt. 24:6.

27. Ps. 24:14.

28. Luke 1:17.

29. Author's emphasis on this prophetic hour as a time of "gathering" for spiritual accounting.

30. Daniel 2.

31. Roger and Sue Mitchell, *Target Europe*. (Kent, England: Sovereign World Publications, 2001).

32. Martin Scott, *Impacting the City*. (Kent, England: Sovereign World Publications, 2003).

33. Ibid., 107.

34. Roger and Sue Mitchell, *Target Europe*. (Kent, England: Sovereign World Publications, 2001), 167.

35. Rev. 2:12-15.

36. John 1:14.

37. Martin Scott, *Impacting the City*. (Kent, England: Sovereign World Publications, 2003), 149.

38. John 10:10.

39. Gen. 5:24.

40. 2 Kings 2.

41. Acts 7:60.

42. Col. 2:14-15.

43. Rev. 12.

44. 2 John 1:7.

45. 1 John 4:3.

46. 1 John 2:22.

47. 1 Cor. 1:18.

48. Dan. 11:32.

49. The Concise Oxford Dictionary Of Current English, New Edition, BCA, 1991

50. Ps. 23:4.

51. John 10:10.

52. Ezek. 37:9.

53. Isa. 42:2-3.

54. Hosea 4:6.

55. John 11:25-26.

56. Matt. 11:11-12.

57. Luke 16:16.

58. Luke 17:21.

59. John 10:10.

60. Isa. 60:2-3.

61. Rev. 2:8.

62. Rev. 2:12.

63. 1 Chron. 4:9.

64. John 15:6.

65. Num. 23:20.

66. Rev. 12:12.

67. Gen. 3:1.

68. Job 22:28.

69. Num. 25.

70. Roger and Sue Mitchell, *Target Europe*. (Kent, England: Sovereign World Publications, 2001), 162.

71. Dan. 9:2-3; Ezra 8:21-23.

72. Roger and Sue Mitchell, *Target Europe*. (Kent, England: Sovereign World Publications, 2001), 162.

73. Ps. 24:1.

74. Martin Scott, *Impacting the City*. (Kent, England: Sovereign World Publications, 2003), 150.

75. Rev. 4:1.

76. 1 Pet. 4:10.

77. John 4:24.

78. Eph. 4:11-16.

79. James 2:17.

80. Matt. 18:19.

81. Ezek. 33.

82. Matt. 11:11-12.

83. John 4:24.

84. Ps. 112:9.

85. Martin Scott, *Impacting the City*. (Kent, England: Sovereign World Publications, 2003), 109.

86. Josh. 3:3.

87. Acts 2:14-39.

88. 2 Pet. 3:9.

89. Judges 5:15.

90. Zech. 3:4-5.

91. Ps. 125:3.

92. Acts 17:6.

93. Luke 24:49; Matt. 28:18; Acts 1:8.

94. Mark 16:20; Acts 19.

95. Mark 9:23-24; Mark 11:24.

96. Isa. 60:1.

97. Gal. 6:7.

98. 1 Pet. 1:5.

99. Eph. 2:20-22.

100. Eph. 1:10.

101. Luke 4:18.

102. Heb. 11:6.

103. Matt. 11:12.

104. Heb. 11:1.

105. Matt. 9:22, Mark 5:34.

106. Matt. 8:26; 14:31.

107. 2 Cor. 5:20.

108. Rev. 4:1.

109. Eph. 4:11.

110. Mark 16:20.

111. 2 Pet. 3:9.

112. 2 Cor. 2:4-5.

113. Acts 16:25-26.

114. 2 Cor. 2:17; Job 22:28.

115. Isa. 60:2-3.

116. Eph. 2:18.

117. Col. 2:14-15.

118. James 1:5.

119. James 2:17.

120. Acts 4:12.

121. Rom. 1:17; 4:17.

122. Heb. 11:6.

123. Matt. 9:36.

124. Matt. 18:33.

125. Mark 6:34.

126. Mark 8:2.

127. Gal. 6:2.

128. Heb. 12:2.

129. Isa. 40:3-5.

130. Luke 3:16.

131. Isa. 43:19.

132. Gal. 5:16-22.

133. Heb. 11:24-26.

134. Rom. 4:17.

135. 1 Cor. 1:18.

136. Amos 3:7.

137. Ps. 24:14.

138. Amos 7:14-15.

139. John 4:23-24.

140. Acts 2:19.

141. Jer. 20:9.

142. Recorded on www.womenarisepray.org. "Dance of the Lord" archived 2004.

143. Highlighted for emphasis.

144. Heb. 11:4-12.

145. Isa. 6:8.

146. Eph. 6:12-13.

147. Eph. 3:10.

148. Luke 10:2.

149. 1 John 4:3.

150. Prov. 19:21; Ps. 33:11.

151. Luke 11:17.

152. Jer. 33:3.

153. Rev. 4:1.

154. Luke 18:1; James 5:16.

155. 2 Cor. 10:3-4.

156. Rev. 12:1-12.

157. 1 Chron. 12:32.

158. Dan. 2:28; 9:2-3.

159. Isa. 28:6.

160. 1 Kings 18:42.

161. Rom. 13:11.

162. Gen. 41:1.

163. Daniel 2.

164. 1 John 4:3.

165. Matt. 12:29.

166. 1 Pet. 2:9.

167. Gal. 6:7.

168. Acts 19:13-16.

169. Isa. 60:1-3.

170. Isa. 60:1.

171. 1 Cor. 14:3.

172. 2 Cor. 3:18.

173. Rev. 22:17.

174. Isa. 9:6.

175. Isa. 53:5.

176. 2 Chron. 20:15.

177. John 3:3.

178. Eph. 4:11-16.

179. 1 Pet. 1:16.

180. Matt. 5:13.

181. Luke 11.

182. Jer. 33:3.

183. John 4:24.

184. John 4:7.

185. Luke 6:12.

186. Matt. 28:19.

187. 1 Chron. 12:32.

188. Jer. 33:3.

189. Eph. 6:18.

190. Eph. 3:10.

191. 2 Cor. 10:3-4.

192. Dan. 10:12-13.

193. Acts 20:37-38.

194. Matt. 12:12.

195. Col. 2:15.

196. Josh. 1:3.

197. Luke 1:80.

198. Rom. 8:19.

199. Jack Deere, *Surprised by His Voice* (Eastbourne, England: Kingsway Publications Ltd, 1996), 45.

200. John 5:19.

201. Acts 1:8.

202. Luke 10:2; Matt. 9:37.

203. Acts 19:11-12.

204. 1 Sam. 16:14.

205. Gal. 5:19.

206. Exod. 3:10.

207. 2 Cor. 4:7.

208. 2 Cor. 10:4.

209. Ibid.

210. Mark 16:16-20.

211. Amos 3:8.

212. 1 Cor. 14:3.

213. 1 Cor. 12:4-7.

214. 1 Cor. 13:1.

215. Rom. 8:26-27.

216. 1 Cor. 14:18.

217. 1 Cor. 14:13-15.

218. Ps. 133:1-3.

219. 1 Sam. 26:11.

220. 1 Cor. 2:4.

221. Amos 3:8.

222. Amos 3:7.

223. Ezek. 13:9.

224. 1 Kings 17:1.

225. 2 Sam. 7:4; 1 Kings 17:2.

226. Neh. 2:1.

227. Dan. 2:47.

228. Mal. 4:6.

229. Mal. 3:2-3.

230. Joel 2:28; Acts 2.

231. Acts 2:2.

232. 1 Pet. 4:10.

233. 1 Thess. 5:21; John 4:1.

234. Rom. 12:2.

235. Eph. 1:18.

236. Acts 3:2.

237. 1 Cor. 14:8.

238. 1 Cor. 14:3.

239. Eph. 5:16.

240. Acts 2:2-4.

241. Gal. 6:9.

242. Jack Deere, *The Beginner's Guide to the Gift of Prophecy* (Ann Arbor, Michigan: Servant Publications, 2001), 31.

243. Mike Bickle, *Growing in the Prophetic* (CITY: Kingsway Publications Eastbourne, 1998), 109.

244. 1 John 5:6.

245. Luke 4:18.

246. Eph. 4:11-16.

247. Jer. 23:16; 14:14; 1 John 4:1; 1 Thess. 5:20-21.

248. 1 Cor. 14:40.

249. Jer. 23:29.

250. Eph. 4:12.

251. Eph. 4:13-16.

252. Eph. 2:19.

253. Eph. 2: 20.

254. John 4:9.

255. Isa. 5:13; Ezek. 22:26.

256. Eccles. 3:14; Rev. 22:18-19.

257. 2 Tim. 2:15.

258. Acts 17:11.

259. Acts 15:32 and Jer. 1:1-12.

260. Hos. 4:6.

261. Phil. 3:12-13.

262. Amos 3:3.

263. 1 Cor. 14:26,29,32.

264. 2 Tim. 2:4.

265. Acts 21:9.

266. Exod. 4:12.

267. Dan. 1:17.

268. Jer. 1:5.

269. Eph. 4:10-16; Eph. 2:20-22.

270. Mark 16:15.

271. Mark 16:20.

272. 1 Cor. 2:4-5.

273. Rom. 8:19.

274. Luke 2:49.

275. Matt. 21:14.

276. John 11:43.

277. John 6.

278. Mark 6:46.

279. Matt. 9:35-36.

280. Mark 16:15.

281. Matt. 28:19.

282. Rom. 8:1-2; 2 Cor. 5:17.

283. John 14:12.

284. John 4.

285. Mark 16:15; Matt. 28:19.

286. Ps. 125:3.

287. Matt. 12:21-23.

288. 1 Thess. 5:24.

289. Acts 9:15.

290. 1 Kings 17:9.

291. 1 Kings 18:21.

292. 1 Kings 17:1.

293. Acts 13:10-12.

294. James 1:2-3.

295. Dan. 10:12-13.

296. Dan. 10:20.

297. Acts 19:35.

298. Acts 13:4-12.

299. Acts 19:14.

300. Jer. 1:4-5.

301. Col. 4:6.

302. Jer. 9:23-24.

303. Job 5:17.

304. Daniel 9, 10.

305. Mic. 2:13.

306. Hos. 4:6.

307. Jer. 33:3.

308. Segun Johnson, Roger Mitchell, Samuel Rhein, Micheal Schiffmann and Chris Seaton, *Unscrambling Africa* (Peaceworks Publications, 2005), 14.

309. Isa. 40:3.

310. Rev. 19:10.

311. 1 John 4:2-3.

312. 1 Cor. 14:1.

313. Dan. 10:12-13.

314. 1 Tim. 1:18.

315. Rom. 12:6.

316. Author's emphasis.

317. Jim W. Goll, *The Seer*, (Shippensburg, PA, USA: Destiny Image Publishers, 2004), 34.

318. 1 John 4:8.

319. Joel 2:28-32; Acts 2:17.

320. Rom. 8:19.

321. Eph. 6:12.

322. Luke 11:21-23.

323. Exod. 2:14.

324. Exod. 2:15.

325. Exod. 3:3.

326. Exod. 3:14.

327. Gen. 29:27.

328. Gen. 31:13.

329. 1 Sam. 17:39.

330. 1 Sam. 17:49.

331. Dan. 1:8.

332. Dan. 3:25.

333. Dan. 6:22.

334. 1 Kings 18:30.

335. Neh. 2:19.

BIBLIOGRAPHY

Bickle, Mike. *Growing In The Prophetic*. East Sussex, UK: Kingsway Publications LTD, 1995.

Conner, Kevin J. *The Church In The New Testament*. Kent, England: Sovereign World International, 1982.

Dance of the Lord. www.womenarisepray.org. Word for Israel and the Church.

Deere, Jack. *Surprised By The Voice Of God*. Grand Rapids, MI: Zondervan Publishing House, 1996.

Deere, Jack. *The Beginner's Guide to the Gift of Prophecy*. Ann Arbor, MI: Servant Publications, 2001.

Goll, Jim W. *The Seer*. Shippensburg, PA, USA: Destiny Image Publishers Inc., 2004.

Johnson Segun, Roger Mitchell, Samuel Rhein, Micheal Schiffmann and Chris Seaton. *Unscrambling Africa*. Bognor Regis, UK: Peaceworks Publications, 2005.

Mitchell, Roger and Sue. *Target Europe*. Kent, UK: Sovereign World Ltd, 2001.

Pax-Harry, Obii. *Developing Passion For The Prophetic*. Birmingham, UK: Arise Missions Publications, 2004. Self published manual.

Pax-Harry, Obii. *Word For the Decade & Beyond*. Edited & Published by Patrick Stevenson, 2004. Self published manual.

Scott, Martin. *Impacting the City*. Kent, UK: Sovereign World Ltd, 2004.

Yoder, Barbara J. *The Breaker Anointing*. Colorado Springs, CO: Wagner Publications, 2001.

The Concise Oxford Dictionary Of Current English, New Edition, BCA, 1991.

About the Author

Obii Pax-Harry is a dynamic leader of several prayer, prophetic, and apostolic initiatives in the United Kingdom and other nations. She was used to birth the International Prayer Ministry, Women Arise, with several prayer chapters around the world. Obii also pioneered the Strategic Prayer School (now House of Prayer) Birmingham and Redditch in Partnership with Prayer for the Nations, London. These initiatives have been released into capable hands of prophetic intercessors trained under Obii's mentorship.

Obii's heart is to see the Body of Christ mobilized as an active, influential body doing the works of Christ. In fulfillment of her call to apostolic leadership, she wrote *The New Believers Course*, a 12-week interactive course to prepare the Church for life on the streets; and *How to Exercise your Prophetic Gift* to prepare the Church for life as a Prophetic Bride. She is also the author of *Breakthrough Prayers, Moving to the Next Level, Releasing the Gadites, Issachar Anointing,* and several other training manuals.

Obii has a heart for Christian media, having hosted her own daily radio broadcast "Women Arise" on Talkgospel.com aired by Sky TV Network in 2000. She has also been invited as a guest on several radio and television programs in the United Kingdom. She is an executive member of the Christian Broadcasting Council of Great Britain (CBC), and a columnist for the CBC Magazine, *The New Voice*.

Obii is an ordained minister, currently serving as pastor of the Resurrection Life Assembly in Birmingham, England, with an apostolic team. She is a sought-after international and national conference speaker who ministers with passion with signs and wonders following.

Obii Pax-Harry completed the Solicitors Finals Course in the United Kingdom, but gave up her promising career in law to pursue her dream of raising a family. In 2003, after a revelation from the Lord based on Daniel 7:25, Obii returned to law school to study for a Master of Laws at the University of Birmingham. Obii believes the body of Christ is undergoing a divine shift that is repositioning the physical, mental, and spiritual gifts of believers for the glory of the Kingdom. She is married and has three children.

Additional copies of this book and
other book titles from
DESTINY IMAGE EUROPE
are available at your local bookstore.

We are adding new titles every month!

To view our complete catalog on-line, visit us at:

www.eurodestinyimage.com

Send a request for a catalog to:

Via Acquacorrente, 6
65123 - Pescara - ITALY
Tel. +39 085 4716623 - Fax +39 085 4716622

* * * * * * * * * * * * * * * * * * *
Are you an author?

Do you have a "today" God-given message?

CONTACT US

We will be happy to review your
manuscript for a possible publishing:

publisher@eurodestinyimage.com